Business Planning and Entrepreneurship

Business Planning and Entrepreneurship

An Accounting Approach

Michael Kraten

Business Planning and Entrepreneurship

Copyright © Michael Kraten, 2010.

First published in 2010 by
Business Expert Press, LLC
222 East 46th Street, New York, NY 10017
www.businessexpertpress.com

ISBN-13: 978-1-60649-046-4 (paperback)
ISBN-10: 1-60649-046X (paperback)

ISBN-13: 978-1-60649-047-1 (e-book)
ISBN-10: 1-60649-047-8 (e-book)

DOI 10.4128/9781606490471

A publication in the Business Expert Press Managerial Accounting collection

Collection ISSN (print) 2152-7113
Collection ISSN (electronic) 2152-7121

Cover design by Jonathan Pennell
Interior design by Scribe, Inc.

First edition: February 2010

10 9 8 7 6 5 4 3 2 1

Printed in the United States of America.

Abstract

This text is a nuts-and-bolts guide to business planning. It is designed to function as a handbook for entrepreneurs who wish to apply techniques of management accounting to their planning activities.

Because management accounting is a practical discipline, it provides an ideal framework for the construction of business plans. This book leads the reader through six major sections that represent the modular components of any organizational plan; the reader is encouraged to follow along and construct a plan for his or her own organization as he or she progresses through each chapter.

The six sections address the major topics of the plan, namely: the business model, volume estimation, cost estimation, revenue estimation, investment value, and risk management. Each section is subdivided into three distinct chapters that address the concrete concepts, tools, and techniques of business planning.

The chapters and sections include cross-referenced information in order to help the reader grasp various fundamental principles that pervade all planning documents. For instance, the topic of cost behavior first appears during the discussion of direct and indirect costs in the cost estimation section of the text and is later revisited during the discussion of price targeting in the revenue estimation section. Such linkages help the reader develop plans that are heavily integrated in nature and firmly grounded in content.

Furthermore, this text also integrates management accounting concepts with relevant themes that are shared with other fields of business. Concepts of supply and demand, for instance, are shared by management economists; they are addressed in the volume estimation section of this text. And techniques of competitive pricing strategy are shared by marketing professionals; they are likewise addressed in the revenue estimation section.

Another distinctive element of this text is its coverage of the discipline of risk management, which appears explicitly as the final major section of the book and implicitly as well within earlier sections such as cost variance analysis. Entrepreneurs that are faced with highly uncertain business conditions can benefit by incorporating concepts and techniques of risk management in their plans.

Some readers may wish to focus on the illustrative examples in each chapter that follow the activities of a single entrepreneur as he applies principles of management accounting to his planning activities throughout his large organization. Other readers may choose to refer to the integrated example in the appendix that summarizes the planning activities of a different entrepreneur who is managing a much smaller firm.

All readers, though, can benefit by learning how to use techniques of management accounting to support and strengthen any business plan. This book provides a useful template for such activities.

Keywords

Activity-based costing, business planning, cash flow analysis, competitive pricing, cost behavior, direct costs, financial ratio analysis, flexible budgets, game theory, indirect costs, internal controls, management accounting, outcomes management, outcomes measurement, price discounting, price targeting, process chain, process flow analysis, quality management, risk assessment, risk management, scenario event identification, supply and demand, variance analysis

Contents

PART I

Introduction

CHAPTER 1

Management Accounting and Business Planning

About This Chapter

Chapter 1 explains why entrepreneurs should apply management accounting techniques to their business planning activities. Management accounting is a very practical discipline; it focuses on the nuts-and-bolts of business operations. Thus, when developing the foundations of a business plan, it is important to utilize these techniques in order to demonstrate that management is competent to operate the firm.

Chapters 2 through 19 of this book lead readers through a series of six major sections that encompass the business plan; these sections address the business model, volume estimation, cost estimation, revenue estimation, investment value, and risk management. Chapter 1 (i.e., this chapter) compares these sections to the sections of a building; our book describes how entrepreneurs build their business plans from their foundations up.

This book targets entrepreneurs who already possess a basic level of knowledge of accounting fundamentals but who are unfamiliar with the manner in which critical management accounting techniques should be incorporated into business plans. These readers may find that certain concepts (such as residual income in chapter 15) are completely new to them, while others (such as the use of behavioral cost assumptions to establish pricing strategies in chapter 11) are familiar concepts that are applied in novel ways.

Management Accounting and Business Planning

I need to see a business plan. A practical one, one that tells me that you've thought about the future and you're prepared to deal with it. Please don't take last year's plan and simply roll it forward. And for goodness sake, please don't buy some software off the shelf and simply plug numbers into it.

Do you need to write a *practical* business plan—a nuts-and-bolts document that clearly demonstrates that you're prepared to operate your business from day one? Not one that focuses on theoretical components like mission statements, but one that addresses nitty-gritty issues such as volume, cost, revenue, and investment value?

If your investor, lender, board member, or government regulator is demanding such a plan, then you cannot use any of the standardized management planning software systems that have been commercially developed for the mass market. Such systems have limited flexibility; they will not permit you to customize your material to reflect the unique needs of your organization.

Nor can you simply update your previous year's business plan. The external environment is evolving very quickly, and your internal environment may need to undergo rapid transformations as well. By simply rolling a previous plan forward, you would be rolling forward the status quo.

So where should you turn for guidance in developing a business plan? Fortunately, you have two choices. One choice is to turn to strategic management professionals who will speak to you about long-term market trends; help you analyze your strengths, weaknesses, opportunities, and threats; and then work with you to produce a plan that focuses on your theoretical mission and your future goals.

This is *not* such a plan.

The other choice is to ask a group of management accountants to walk you through your business. Not financial accountants who simply record transactions that have already occurred, but management accountants who roll up their sleeves, get their hands dirty, and help you plan for the future.

This *is* such a plan.

Management accountants tend to think of themselves as architects and construction foremen. Their business plans may not be works of literary art, but they are quite sturdy and stand up well in shifting market conditions. Like strong buildings that are designed to withstand hurricanes and earthquakes, their plans feature solid proverbial foundations, thick walls, and a firm roof. And managerial accountants do not simply complete their work and walk away; instead, they conduct a series of stress tests to ensure that their plans are ready for occupancy before they are placed into use.

The Infrastructure of a Plan

The *foundation* of a plan is an evidence-based description of the business model (part II). It illustrates how the entity will organize itself to produce and distribute products and services that can generate sufficient incoming resources to sustain growth (chapter 2). It also presents statistical evidence that the business model is grounded in reality (chapter 3). Finally, it demonstrates that the model is capable of producing profits—or, at a minimum, producing affordable losses—in bad times as well as good times (chapter 4).

The walls (parts III, IV, and V) of a plan are built upon this foundation, drawing support and data from the preceding information to illustrate the details of the operation. First the *framework* of the walls (part III) is constructed to provide a sense of the scale, scope, and shape of the structure. Then the costly electrical, ventilation, and plumbing *utility systems* are built into the walls (part IV) to support the active use of the building. And finally the drywall and paint *finishing details* are completed (part V) to create a livable environment.

Within a business plan, the framework is the volume estimate, featuring a reconciliation (chapter 7) of production supply (chapter 5) and consumer demand (chapter 6). The utility systems are the cost estimates for all production, distribution, and administration functions (chapters 8 through 10). And the finishing details are the revenue estimates that provide assurance that the organization is able to support itself (chapters 11 through 13).

Next we need a *roof* (part VI) for our plan, which protects the walls and the foundation—essentially providing shelter for the entire entity—by illustrating that all of the activities that were described in previous chapters can generate sufficient investment value to satisfy our sources of capital. Such information should address both quantitative and qualitative considerations and should be expressed in reports that are distributed inside and outside the organization (chapters 14 through 16).

And finally, we need to *stress test* the entire structure (part VII). In other words, we need to be risk managers who self-critique our plan, subjecting it to harsh scrutiny by imagining how we might alter it "on the fly" under the harshest of all plausible future scenarios (chapters 17 through 19).

A Modular Construction Strategy

This book is constructed in a modular format; it is designed to help you move from section to section of your own business plan and plug in the required pieces as you progress through your work. The business model foundation, volume estimate wall framework, cost estimate wall utility systems, revenue estimate wall finishing details, investment value roof, and risk management stress tests are all discussed in a part of this book; each part is divided into three chapters. This introductory chapter, the 18 part chapters, and our concluding chapter provide you with 20 modular documents. If you complete one chapter per day, you can complete this book—and your own business plan—in 4 weeks . . . without working any weekends!

Are we prepared to proceed to our first section? Not quite yet, for each of our chapters is equipped with its own applied business example to support its instructional content. Let us now proceed to our first applied illustration; considering the prominent role of the health care industry in the American economy, we've decided to follow the planning activities of Hugh the home care agency entrepreneur as we progress throughout the book.

Note: The 20 applied illustrations in our 20 chapters follow Hugh as he applies our management accounting techniques to various operating and support divisions within his firm. Please consult the appendix for a unified example of a small start-up business that applies information from all of our chapters to the business plan of a single division firm.

Applied Illustration

Hugh has built a successful home care agency that serves various types of consumers, including a wide variety of geriatric senior citizens as customers. Hugh's firm sends nurses to homes to provide specialty services that are billed directly to consumers and other private payors;

"private pay" billing is required because the services are usually not deemed reimbursable by any government program.

Hugh reviews the introductory information in this chapter and decides to sketch out a few ideas before proceeding to chapter 2. Let's listen in on his thoughts as he approaches his task:

What is my business model? Well, I once believed that my sales (i.e., consumer or customer) representatives should simply go out and sell the clinically complex specialty services that my nurses enjoy developing, but now I've changed my mind. What my customers really want—and what they are willing to pay for—are relatively simple home support services that aren't covered by their government plans. Their preferences change every time the government changes its coverage policy, so my sales force should really be communicating the needs of our consumers to my nurses, not the other way around.

Okay, so my business plan will be organized around my consumers and, by extension, the sales representatives that act as the conduits that synthesize their needs and direct my nurses. Hopefully, our growth will continue in small and steady spurts because we'll continue to expand our service mix each time the government further trims its list of covered services. So I'll need to let my nurses know not to spend time trying to invent a "next generation" specialty service.

I'll ask my consumers to start submitting feedback surveys to complement the information that we receive through our sales representatives. I guess our greatest risk will be a slowdown of business if the government stops trimming their lists of covered services.

Hugh jots down the following:

- Focus on consumer
- Sales representatives drive nurses (reverse the status quo!)
- Small and steady growth from continuing health plan coverage reductions
- Feedback survey evidence

Now let me think about my volume, cost, and revenue estimates. Right now, our consumer demand is just about limitless. The American population is aging rapidly, and new home-based treatments for special diseases and conditions are emerging every day. We're at the "hot spot" of demand growth in both demography and research technology.

And we don't have to worry about our supply of nurses, either; we can hire them overseas if we can't find them here in American schools. But timing is always a problem. It takes time to find qualified nurses overseas, and it's difficult to interview them from here; we incur all sorts of costs in managing a global human resources recruiting team. And sometimes our consumers balk at paying those costs, especially when they learn that we intend to conduct on-the-job training sessions during their home care visits. When that occurs, they accuse us of preparing our nurses to treat future consumers "on their dime."

So our volume estimation process will need to focus on reconciling our local consumer demand with our geographically distant nursing sources. We might need to tweak our pricing strategy to manage that process, perhaps by charging our consumers a premium fee whenever we need to use our costly global network to develop and deliver an extremely labor-intensive level of service. Our consumers won't like paying for that level of service, but if I promise not to conduct on-the-job training sessions "on their dime," they might go for it.

Hugh jots down the following:

- Customer demand limitless in short term
- Nurse supply available but expensive in short term
- Customers may balk at paying premiums for nurses that require training
- Should we offer training restrictions?

Now on to investment value and risk management. There isn't much to say here because I haven't built my home care agency's foundations and walls yet. But it seems pretty obvious that our investment value is going to be driven qualitatively by consumer satisfaction and quantitatively by cash flow—in other words, by being able to charge and collect enough in revenues to find and pay nurses quickly to meet our consumers' short-term demands.

Stress tests? I can't imagine that the world will run out of nurses any time soon, or that home care services will suddenly become unnecessary. But I am concerned about how we'd survive if the government stops trimming their lists of covered services each year.

Hugh jots down the following:

- Consumer satisfaction creates value
- Collect premium fees for services rendered to consumers
- Demand driven by covered-service decisions by insurers . . . a big risk!

Looking Forward

In this chapter, we explained how management accounting applications add value during the business planning process. We also employed the metaphor of a building to describe how six specific sections—in other words, those encompassing the business model, volume estimation, cost estimation, revenue estimation, investment value, and risk management—can be used to construct a plan.

In the next chapter, we begin our exploration of three management accounting applications involving the business model. We start with the activity of defining the process chain, following Hugh (as we will continue to do throughout this book) during his efforts in applying business planning techniques to issues concerning his home care agency.

PART II
The Business Model

CHAPTER 2

Defining the Process Chain

About This Chapter

Chapter 2 begins our exploration of the business model by describing how entrepreneurs should define their process chains. Any successful organization should be able to state, clearly and concisely, how they engage competent employees to perform their tasks well, thereby enhancing sales revenue and thus increasing operating profits and cash flows.

At this initial stage of the business planning process, our material is completely conceptual in nature. Nevertheless, this conceptual information serves as the foundation for the sizable amounts of quantitative detail that follow throughout the business plan.

Although many components of a business plan are confidential, entrepreneurs should keep in mind that the process chain often serves an important role in public relations campaigns. In other words, all of the constituents of the firm—employees, managers, customers, and investors—often respond positively to information about how their collaborative activities create successful enterprises.

Defining the Process Chain

Let's start by helping me understand the building blocks of your business strategy. Whom are you relying on? What are they going to do? How are you going to get noticed and appreciated? And why should anyone give you money to build your organization?

Success is often determined by an ability to *focus* on a small number of critical success factors. Organizations, like people, should *focus* on these factors when performing the work that results in the production and delivery of goods and services.

Amazingly, though, some organizations don't even bother to identify their critical success factors. Others do so, but they fail to measure their own rates of success in performing these tasks. And yet others neglect to obtain continuous feedback from customers and investors, information that they need to continually refocus on the most important elements of their business model.

These organizations, of course, are bound to *fail*. Other organizations, such as those that identify, measure, and continually revise their critical success factors, are bound to *succeed*.

So how does an organization begin to define these building blocks of the business model? First it must construct its *process chain*; then it must identify the *four elements* of the chain.

The Process Chain

There are huge firms and tiny firms, global firms and local firms, for-profit firms and nonprofit firms. And yet they all share one feature in common: They all must focus on the same number of elements in their process chains—namely, four elements.

At the most fundamental level, all successful organizations produce value by mastering a simple sequence of events. They find good *people* . . . who do good *work* . . . thus pleasing their *consumers* . . . resulting in the receipt of funds from *purchasers and investors*. Only the specifics of each element of this chain may vary from organization to organization; the sequence, though, is a universal one.

Some people think of this *process chain* as a simple common sense description of business operations. But when they proceed to define each element, they realize that their task can become rather complicated.

The Four Elements

Good *people*—that is, employees who are well educated and highly motivated to learn and grow along with the organization—form the foundation of any successful business. But how do we identify the most important people in our firm? And might our choice evolve as the firm changes over time?

In the previous chapter, our friend Hugh concluded that his most important employees were his consumer representatives and not his nurses. Similarly, in luxury retail stores, the meagerly paid floor assistants are sometimes more valuable than the back-office managers. And yet high-volume, low-margin retailers might rely more on their merchandise buying staff than on their floor sales staff for their success. In fact, competitors who battle each other in a single industry might adopt very different strategies and thus might emphasize very different categories of employees.

Good people must *work* efficiently and effectively in order to help the organization achieve its goals. But they cannot succeed without being furnished with the training materials, the tools of the trade, and the managerial guidance that they require in order to complete their tasks.

Some organizations require their employees to spend their working lives cycling endlessly through meeting after meeting, producing no output of any meaningful value to customers or sources of financial capital. Other firms, though, place themselves in position to succeed by listening to their workers to understand what they really need to do their jobs . . . and then by holding their workers accountable for producing excellent work once they obtain the support that they have requested.

But these are internal concerns; what about the external market? When gas-guzzling automobiles pile up in dealership lots during times of high gasoline prices, or when seats in university classrooms go unfilled while online course slots are oversubscribed, such conditions serve as indicators that organizations have lost touch with the needs of their own *consumers*. They might continue to employ good people who produce quality work, but if such work fails to result in consumer satisfaction and sales, the activity expended is all for naught.

It is important to recognize that some consumers are more valuable to organizations than others, and that the identity of the most valuable consumer group(s) may evolve over time. Many foreign automobile companies, for instance, initially focused on budget consumers when they first entered the American market and then moved up to more affluent consumers over time. Similarly, many colleges grow into full-fledged universities as they add graduate degree programs, and then postgraduate executive education programs, to their original undergraduate offerings.

But how is capital acquired to make these processes possible? Unless an organization is *cash flow positive* and can afford to finance all of its current and future business development activities out of operating earnings, it will need to rely on investors, lenders, grantors, and other sources of external capital to support its growth. In fact, even if there is no need for any sources of external capital, an organization will still need to ensure that its existing owners are satisfied with the returns on their original investments.

Many organizations fail to recognize and pursue lucrative sources of new financial capital. Others, though, recognize that their own consumers may lead them in the direction of such opportunities. Certain high-end department store chains, for instance, attract venture capitalists as investors after catering to them as customers for many years. And many nonprofit universities transform their staid endowment funds into aggressive hedge funds after hiring alumni of their own finance programs.

Applied Illustration

Hugh is proud of the success that he has realized in developing his home care agency from "scratch." From the moment that he opened for business 5 years ago, and for a period of 4 consecutive years, he rode a boom in the expansion of demand for health services to a series of increasing annual profits. A recent decline in demand due to retrenchments in wealth, though, has compelled him to adopt a more rigorous approach to business planning.

Hugh decides to flesh out a description of his process chain to analyze some changes that he has been considering about his business strategy. Let's follow his stream of thought as he works his way through the four elements of his analysis.

I once thought that our most valuable employees are the senior clinicians who supervise the caregivers, keep abreast of industry trends, and pursue new market opportunities. But then I started to analyze our profits on a cross-sectional basis, and I realized that I am actually losing money on consumers who utilize the medically intensive services that reflect the "cutting edge" technological developments of our industry. On the other hand, I earn huge profits on consumers who require relatively simple caregiver services like home-based physical and occupational therapy; they allow me to hire relatively inexperienced and inexpensive staff and to schedule many brief visits each day instead of a few lengthy ones.

So I suppose that our most valuable employees are the consumer representatives who perform our marketing, public relations, and outreach activities, and who can identify consumers that might benefit from home-based therapies. But to perform their work activities well, our representatives need to know where these consumers congregate and how they can be persuaded to attend "information sessions," which means developing a database that highlights the names and characteristics of regular visitors at diners, senior centers, church establishments, and so on. And our representatives should be given mobile data-entry devices with Internet access so they can enroll prospective consumers on the spot.

Hugh jots down the following:

- Drivers of success: home-based therapies
- Key people: consumer representatives
- Work activities focus on instant enrollment at information sessions

My high-priority customer group? That's an easy one to identify: mentally active seniors with physical ailments, of course! In particular, we should focus on consumers who wish to remain physically active but who experience limited mobility due to arthritis, vision degeneration, and similar conditions. Those are the individuals who are most eager to sign up for physical and occupational therapies.

Seniors like to spend time with other seniors, so perhaps I should hire a few physically active septuagenarians who need a part-time salary and can easily relate to my target market. And now that I'm transitioning our business model in this direction, I should ask our local business partners to refer us to a geriatric social worker who can help train our staff.

Hugh jots down the following:

- Key customers: mentally active seniors with limited mobility
- Consider enhanced employee hires and training

Many of my best referral sources run diners and get to know their customers well; I wonder whether they might be willing to collaborate with me by developing monthly "health event" lunches for seniors. Right now, they simply allow me to rent private rooms and buy lunch for seniors while distributing literature, but if I can "jazz up" the agendas by bringing in popular guest speakers and adding some fun activities, I might be able to attract seniors who aren't regular diner customers. If that's the case, then the diner owners might be willing to waive the rental fees and become partners instead of landlords.

Hugh jots down the following:

- Diner owners as referral sources *and* business partners
- Develop monthly health events to attract new customers

Okay, let's summarize our process chain. How will (a) my most valuable employees (b) work efficiently and effectively to (c) delight my most valuable target consumers and thus (d) attract the interest of diner owners? Well, I'll focus on turning my consumer representatives into mobile ambassadors at various community locations, which will require some new investment in training and equipment. And I'll kill two birds with one stone by finding diner owners within my own network; they can partner with me to attract new consumers to each of our businesses while (hopefully) reducing or eliminating their room rental fees.

Looking Forward

In this chapter, we explained how the concept of the process chain can help entrepreneurs focus on the critical factors that determine organizational success. We described a chain of four specific factors—the employees we hire, the work they perform, the consumers we attract, and the investors or partners who finance our capital requirements—that represent the building blocks of a successful business strategy.

In the next chapter, we continue our development of the process chain by collecting and evaluating statistical evidence that reveals whether our strategy is functioning (or will be able to function) in an effective manner. In other words, in chapter 3, we move beyond the conceptual definitions of the process chain and begin to work with quantitative measurements involving the four factors.

CHAPTER 3

Justifying the Process Chain With Statistical Evidence

About This Chapter

Chapter 3 continues our exploration of the business model by describing how entrepreneurs should collect and analyze data to support their process chains. They accomplish these tasks by identifying key relationships, defining causal and effect variables, collecting data in quantitative format from a representative sample, and analyzing the information in a statistically valid manner.

At this early stage of the business planning process, the quantitative data are nonfinancial in nature. Nevertheless, the analytical conclusions that are drawn from the data support the financial details that follow throughout the business plan.

Although the conceptual components of the process chain are often publicly known, the statistical evidence that justifies the chain is usually treated in a highly confidential manner. For obvious reasons, organizations would not want their customers or competitors to know when (and how) their own statistical evidence draws doubt upon the validity of their business models.

Justifying the Process Chain With Statistical Evidence

Your process chain seems reasonable to me, but are you sure that it reflects reality? You're making some important assumptions about how your people, your work activities, your customers, and your investment strategies influence each other. That's not just speculation, is it?

The process chain kicks off the business plan with a purely theoretical description of the organization's strategic model. A theoretical opening section serves a valid purpose; after all, readers need to understand how our processes are designed before they proceed to the quantitative details.

And thus, in this chapter, we do exactly that; we focus on the quantitative details. Now that we have compiled a description of the relationships between the four elements of the process chain, we must seek to confirm the validity of these relationships in some statistical fashion.

How do we do that? To put it simply, we ask a lot of questions and collect a lot of measurements. Then we use a statistical program to generate a correlation analysis. Finally, if the correlations look reasonable, we generate a more advanced statistical analysis that searches for missing variables.

Defining Our Variables

Some business managers believe that the most important step of any statistical analysis isn't the collection of the data or the analysis of the results; instead, it's the definition of the variables. "Garbage in, garbage out," they argue, implying that a weak set of definitions will inevitably produce a meaningless set of conclusions.

Looking back at the process chain, it becomes evident that some of the relationships between the elements are more important than others. In a customer-focused retail business that emphasizes luxurious surroundings, for instance, the most important relationship might be the one between the customer and the retail environment. But in a back-office technology service business that emphasizes the inexpensive, reliable, and automated completion of millions of computerized tasks, the most important relationship might be the one between the software programmers and the system itself.

We need to select the *key relationship* and define it in a variable format. Then, for the sake of argument, we need to define some plausible *alternative relationships* as well. For instance, we may ask, "Will superior customer service lead to increased sales? Or will customers be more impressed by the range of our product line? Or will they simply make their purchasing decisions on the basis of price?" Our first step is thus the definition of the *causal variables* (in this case, service, product range, and price) and the *effect variable* (in this case, the customer's purchasing intention).

Collecting Our Data

Once we define our variables, we need to select a *sample* of individuals, items, or practices—whatever it is that we are measuring—and collect our data. But the sample itself needs to be *representative* of the elements of our process chain, and the data must be collected in a *format* that lends itself to statistical analysis.

The representation requirement is a simple one; if we plan to ask frail senior citizens about their intention to purchase a device that helps them remain mobile, for instance, it wouldn't make much sense to include their grandchildren in our sample. But we might want to include a few adult children, and perhaps a few caregivers as well, if these individuals influence the buying decisions of our target market.

The data format requirement is a more subtle one; it requires that *word* answers be shunned and *numerical* answers be utilized. "What is your favorite clothing color?" for instance, would yield responses that cannot be analyzed in a quantitative fashion. You'd generate more useful data if you ask a question like "Think about the ROYGBIV (i.e., red, orange, yellow, green, blue, indigo, and violet) spectrum of color. If red is 1, green is 4, and violet is 7, what number best reflects your favorite clothing color?"

Analyzing Our Results

Once we collect our data, we can copy it into a statistical analysis program to learn whether our results are consistent with the most important relationship in our process chain. Some business professionals hire PhDs to produce unbelievably complex analyses; we'll present a useful yet basic analysis instead in our following applied business example.

There are a few important matters to keep in mind as we review that example. First, our goal is to learn whether the causal variable that we emphasize in our process chain really appears to affect our effect variable. And second, we need to ascertain whether there is some other causal variable out there—something we haven't considered—that may be affecting our effect variable as well. If that's the case, then we might need to brainstorm a bit to identify those additional causal variables.

Finally, we should never assume that we can prove cause-and-effect relationships based on statistical data alone. We might notice, for instance, that each time the weather forecaster on the morning news warns us of a blizzard, we inevitably experience a few inches of snow (or perhaps much more) later that day. Statistically speaking, it would appear that the forecaster's prediction actually causes the storm. It would be a mistake, though, to assume that we could create snowstorms on demand by simply asking the forecaster to predict them.

Applied Illustration

There is new competition in town, and Hugh is concerned. A large out-of-state health services corporation, one possessing longstanding referral relationships with major health plans, has established a small pilot office in the region; it has begun offering cut-rate prices to gain a market toehold. Hugh decides to emphasize his homegrown community roots to protect his firm from this new threat.

However, Hugh has begun to worry that a weakening economic environment might persuade health plans to encourage his consumers to try the lower-priced provider; he decides to invite 10 consumers to a focus group session to investigate his concerns. Although he believes that his process chain should always emphasize consumer education through well-trained sales representatives, he is concerned that health plans might start prodding his clientele toward low-cost, mass-market, impersonal alternatives by offering to waive certain copayments and other out-of-pocket costs.

So Hugh asks ten representative consumers,

> *On a scale of 1 to 10, how important is the quality of the agency and its caregivers to you? How about the cost? And, just to play devil's advocate, how about the attractiveness of any freebies—like free caps and shirts—that you may receive from health plans or providers?*

Hugh collects their answers and copies them into a simple table (see Table 3.1), along with the number of therapy visits that each consumer received from his agency last year.

Table 3.1.

Quality	Cost	Freebies	Visits
1	7	5	10
9	2	9	99
2	5	3	32
6	5	2	59
5	6	4	51
5	5	0	40
8	3	8	68
9	2	1	90
8	2	5	81
3	7	8	21

Hugh's business strategy is based on the assumption that high-volume consumers will care deeply about quality but not about cost. Thus, large numbers in the "visits" column should be matched with large numbers in the "quality" column and small numbers in the "cost" column. But does the data reflect Hugh's assumption?

Hugh copies the table into a common spreadsheet program, clicks on the "Data Analysis" choice in the menu, and runs three distinct *correlation analyses*. In other words, three times in succession, he takes a causal variable (i.e., "quality," "cost," and "freebies") and matches it with the effect variable "visits." (*Note: All major spreadsheet programs offer the ability to run correlation analyses; please use the "Help" function in your version of your spreadsheet program if you are unable to locate it easily.*)

What are the results of his analyses? Hugh finds that the correlation of "quality" with "visits" is +0.95, the correlation of "cost" with "visits" is −0.93, and the correlation of "freebies" with "visits" is +0.10. Knowing that each correlation (r) is expressed on a 0.000 to 1.000 basis, Hugh understands how to interpret these results. His highest volume customers respond strongly and positively to quality; they barely respond at all to freebies. Hugh is satisfied that these results are consistent with his agency's business strategy, but at first he is worried about the large correlation between "cost" and "visits."

And then he notices the minus sign in front of the "cost" correlation, and he breathes a sigh of relief. *Of course*, he exclaims, *when health plans offer to waive copayments to steer consumers to low-cost providers, my consumers aren't interested. They might be interpreting low prices as indicators of shoddy services; my representatives have trained my consumers to beware of bargains.*

The negative sign reflects a strong negative relationship between cost levels and sales. But it's not true that Hugh's customers *dislike* low prices (after all, no one does!); it's just that they tend to equate low prices with poor quality.

Hugh jots down the following:

- Consumers strongly value quality (whew!)
- Price negatively correlated with sales . . . not a causal relationship
- Freebies virtually irrelevant

Hugh then assesses whether he might have overlooked any causal variables that influence his customers. He returns to his spreadsheet and runs a *statistical regression analysis*. Because this type of analysis is designed to address the possibility that the collection of causal variables (i.e., "quality," "cost," and "freebies") is incomplete, Hugh runs a single analysis that encompasses all three variables simultaneously.

What are the results of this analysis? Hugh finds that the value of R Square is 0.95. Knowing that correlations are expressed on a 0.000 to 1.000 basis, Hugh understands how to interpret this result: The three causal variables collectively account for 95% of the variation in his customer's purchasing decisions. (*Note: R Square can alternatively be calculated through a series of calculations that compute and compare the combined variations of the causal variables to the overall variation in the effect variable. All introductory statistics textbooks describe these calculations at length.*)

Though Hugh hasn't quite accounted for 100% of the variation, 95% is good enough! He thus concludes that his business model remains valid in the current economic environment.

Hugh jots down the following:

- Only 5% of purchasing decision driven by other causes
- Model is confirmed!

Looking Forward

In this chapter, we explained how entrepreneurs can gather and analyze statistical data to justify the key concepts of their process chains. We also described how correlation and statistical regression analyses can be used to determine whether fundamental assumptions about key relationships are, in fact, valid. Interestingly, even very small focus groups of customers can generate significant information about the soundness of an organization's business strategy.

In the next chapter, we conclude our discussion of the business model by describing how flexible budgeting techniques can be used to assess profitability. In other words, in chapter 4, we move beyond the nonfinancial factors and variables of the process chain and begin to work with financial measurements of success.

CHAPTER 4

Assessing Preliminary Profitability With Flexible Budgets

About This Chapter

Chapter 4 concludes our exploration of the business model by describing how entrepreneurs assess the potential profitability of their enterprises with flexible budgets. Instead of simply preparing a single "most likely" profit budget, it is appropriate to create three distinct budgets, with assumptions ranging from relative pessimism to relative optimism.

The "bottom lines" of each of the three budgets should be compared to the expectations of the organization as a whole. A loss in the pessimistic scenario budget might be acceptable, for instance, if the entity is a small start-up division within a large and wealthy firm. But a profit in the optimistic scenario might be unacceptable if it falls far short of the expectations of shareholders.

At this stage of the business plan, entrepreneurs have not yet completed their in-depth analyses of volumes, costs, and revenues in parts III, IV, and V. Thus, the flexible budgets should be considered "preliminary" in nature—in other words, they are initial "first drafts" to be further refined in the later sections of the plan.

Assessing Preliminary Profitability With Flexible Budgets

Okay, I acknowledge that you've developed a promising business model, and your preliminary data supports your assumptions. But are you sure that you'll be able to survive the bad times in order to enjoy the good times? We all hit rough patches now and then; will you be able to handle them?

Many businesses can achieve their profit goals at some specific level of activity, but they often fall far short of their goals at other levels of activity. For instance, a sparkling new convention center might seem like a great idea for generating local business traffic when the economy is soaring during a period of prosperity, but it can quickly become a barren "white elephant" during a recession. Likewise, a single-site fast food franchise owner might run an incredibly profitable operation when he can personally supervise all activities 18 hours a day, but his profits might sink if he attempts to open a second or third location without hiring additional managers.

A city that is financing a convention center project, as well as a franchise owner who is contemplating the development of a second or third location, might take objection to these comments. "I don't expect to make money all the time," they might argue, "and it's unfair to criticize my plans by noting that I might occasionally hit a rough patch. After all, everyone does so at some point!"

That is certainly true, but business planners need to assess whether the rough patches may actually be capable of bankrupting the entire enterprise. Planners should also assess whether the profits that can be earned in good times will be sufficient to carry the organization through the inevitable bad times.

Some business planners make the mistake of creating a single budget that presents the most likely future scenario of the organization. Under normal circumstances, that budget usually assumes the existence of relatively moderate economic conditions. But such a budget cannot possibly address the *rough patches versus good times* issues that must be assessed as well.

A Three-Scenario Budget

Some organizations use spreadsheet or data base technologies to create dozens of prospective budgets on the basis of numerous sets of simulation assumptions. That approach can certainly produce helpful information, but similar results can often be achieved by creating no more than three—yes, simply three!—discrete budgets.

The first of the three budgets usually reflects the *most likely* scenario. Under normal economic conditions, this might be expected to feature a reasonable level of profit, though the definition of reasonableness might vary with the industry and the strength of the market. Over the long term, though, the profits earned under this scenario must be sufficient to satisfy the expectations of the investors and other contributors of capital funds.

The second of the three budgets usually reflects, somewhat gloomily, the *pessimistic* scenario. Under difficult economic conditions, this might be expected to feature a relatively low level of volume and commensurately low profits, or even significant losses. Although bankruptcy might not necessarily be predicted if the possibility of such a dire occurrence is extremely remote, a painful loss as a result of a steep recession may represent an appropriate forecast here. Under such circumstances, the business planner must question whether (and how) the loss may be financed through credit lines, emergency loans, sales leaseback transactions, or other means of enhancing cash flow.

The third of the three budgets usually reflects, somewhat cheerfully, the *optimistic* scenario. Under highly prosperous economic conditions, this might be expected to feature a relatively high level of volume and correspondingly high profits. But such results should not be taken for granted, for over the long term, the profits that are earned during these times (as well as during normal economic times) will be utilized to repay the capital that is borrowed or otherwise received during recessionary times.

Because the *bottom line* profits or losses in any given period will impact a firm's prospects over the long term, probabilities of occurrence should be annotated to each budget scenario. For instance, if *optimistic period* profits will be used to repay emergency loans that are required to finance *pessimistic period* losses, and if pessimistic periods are expected to occur 20% of the time, then it would be helpful (and perhaps necessary) for optimistic periods to occur at least 20% of the time as well. However, if the optimistic period profits are projected to be twice as large as the pessimistic period losses in absolute terms, optimistic periods would only need to occur at least 10% of the time.

Applied Illustration

Hugh is delighted about a new business development opportunity. Although he was unable to convince any diner owners to allow him to stage health events in their establishments, a major health insurer learned of his proposal and suggested that he consider staging such events in their public conference center. The insurer suggested that they might be able to sell modestly priced tickets for such events and might be able to earn additional revenues from selling video recordings as well.

Let's assume that Hugh can easily stage 16 such events each year. With a little difficulty, if demand is sufficiently high, he will probably be able to stage four additional events each year. And if demand is extremely high, at the very most, he might be able to manage four additional events.

What about event revenues and expenses? Well, let's assume that Hugh expects to average $420 per event in ticket revenue and another $420 per event in video sales revenue. Furthermore, on an annual basis, he expects to receive $8,400 from the government as public service grant revenue. He expects to spend $12,000 on salaries and $14,000 on event liability insurance. Finally, he expects to spend a mere $5 per event on office supplies.

Now let's assume that the health insurer agrees to allow Hugh to sign local advertising deals as long as they do not feature other firms that offer health insurance. So let's assume that Hugh expects to launch two advertising campaigns and plans to add two sharply focused campaigns if there is demand for more than 16 events. Each ad campaign costs $1,000 for production and placement services and each generates earnings of $2,100 from local businesses who contract for the *product placement* insertion of their brand names and logos directly into the ads.

At the beginning of the year, before Hugh knows the level of strength of consumer demand, he creates the following *flexible budget* (see Table 4.1).

Hugh jots down the following:

- Normal demand for 16 events will lead to losses
- But demand for only four additional events will lead to profits

The probabilities of each scenario are extremely difficult to determine, but Hugh understands that it is important to estimate the odds

Table 4.1.

	16 events	20 events	24 events
Grant revenue	8,400	8,400	8,400
Ticket revenue	6,720	8,400	10,080
Video revenue	6,720	8,400	10,080
Product placement revenue	4,200	8,400	8,400
Supplies expense	−80	−100	−120
Salaries expense	−12,000	−12,000	−12,000
Insurance expense	−14,000	−14,000	−14,000
Ad production expense	−2,000	−4,000	−4,000
Net profit	−2,040	3,500	6,840

that each prospective budget may occur. Based on market information that Hugh has collected from his consumer representatives, Hugh estimates the probability of the 16-event scenario as 75%. He estimates the probability of the 20-game scenario as 12.5%. Thus, the probability of the 24-game scenario is also 12.5%.

Hugh then decides to take a "quick cut" at the total profits that he might expect to earn across an 8-year period. He says, *6 years of losing $2,040, 1 year of earning $3,500, and 1 year of earning $6,840 . . . my goodness, that works out to a loss of $1,900!*

At first, he is very worried about his financial prospects. But then he starts to notice certain nuances that make him feel more comfortable with his situation:

> *If I can simply convert 1 of the 6 losing years to a 20-event year, I can swing a $2,040 loss to a $3,500 gain in that year. That's a $5,540 swing in profits; it's more than enough to eliminate my long-term $1,900 loss. After that, any additional improvements in performance would produce even greater total profits.*
>
> *I guess the real question is whether I believe that we are merely going to experience modest demand over the next 8 years, which is the assumption that my $1,900 cumulative loss is based on, or whether I think we might experience demand that is slightly higher. We only need to host 24 events once in 8 years and host 20 events two additional*

times during that time span to swing a profit. That doesn't sound very difficult to me.

My real concern is the $14,000 that I need to spend each year on event liability insurance. Some of my friends who are staging similar events for other health insurers have told me that those firms also underwrite event liability insurance, and thus those policies are made available to them at a nominal cost of $1 per event. My goodness, if I had a deal like that, I could earn a greater amount of net profits by staging 16 events than I can earn today by staging 24 events!

Nevertheless, if all we need to do is perform slightly better than average, then I think we can be profitable over the long term. Perhaps I should think about securing a $10,000 line of credit, in case we only stage 16 events a few years in a row and incur losses of $2,040 each year.

Hugh jots down the following:

- The probabilities of experiencing high demand are relatively strong
- Making this business a reasonable risk if the losses can be financed

Looking Forward

In this chapter, we explained how entrepreneurs can use flexible budgets to estimate, on a preliminary basis, whether they can expect their organizations to remain profitable under varying circumstances. This task is important to the development of the business model because the model itself would need to be modified if there is little or no probability of profits under most circumstances.

In the next chapter, we proceed to our discussion of volume estimation by extending the process chain into a process flow analysis. In other words, in chapter 5, we move beyond our preliminary analyses and begin to develop the volume foundation of our financial statements.

PART III
Volume Estimation

CHAPTER 5

Estimating Supply Capacity With Process Flow Analysis

About This Chapter

Chapter 5 begins our review of the volume estimation section by explaining how process flow analysis can be utilized to quantify production or service capacity. This analytical technique requires business planners to (a) describe their activities in a storyboard format, (b) add target volume estimates for each resource utilized and for each finished good or service produced under a "normal conditions" assumption, and (c) expand each significant target into a range to account for "challenging conditions."

The information that was included in the process chain analysis (see chapter 2) should serve as the basis of this process flow analysis. The resource and finished good volume estimates produced in this section should, in turn, serve as the respective bases of the cost (see part IV) and revenue (see part V) estimates.

Estimating Supply Capacity With Process Flow Analysis

Your flexible budget looks reasonable, but will you actually be able to reach your volume estimates? Even your pessimistic scenario assumes a significant amount of volume; I'm worried that you might fall short of your goals.

Many organizations purchase business interruption insurance policies to cover losses from catastrophic events. When labor strikes, killer hurricanes, and violent political demonstrations wreak havoc on production, such policies can help firms survive abnormally challenging times.

But what about *normally* challenging times? How do firms keep their production lines flowing and their distribution networks busy when deliveries arrive late, machinery breaks down, employees call in sick, and the storage area overflows? Or when a customer calls at the last second and cancels a large order because of a cancellation from his or her own customer? These aren't *abnormal* challenges; these are *normal* challenges. How do firms ensure that they can produce a sufficient level of goods and services?

To answer these questions, a business planner needs to develop a process flow analysis—one that describes all available resources and estimates what can actually be produced from them.

Storyboarding

When film directors first visualize the plots of their films, they often draw sequences of box sketches in comic book format to communicate their plans to others. Business managers complete similar tasks when they begin their process flow analyses.

How do they do so? Step by step, from beginning to end. Any business process begins with the acquisition and temporary storage of raw materials. Laborers then use equipment to transform the materials into finished goods through a series of production activities; after, they place the goods in temporary storage until they are distributed to customers.

Service organizations storyboard their activities in similar fashion. At a hospital emergency room, for instance, the materials are the sick patients who seek care, the laborers are the doctors and nurses, and the production activities are the medical procedures that (hopefully) transform the patients into healthy people. The finished goods are thus the discharged patients who are "stored" temporarily in the lobby until someone takes them home.

A storyboard delineates these details in a step-by-step manner and notes any legal or regulatory constraints that would affect the flow of work. If the legal waiting area capacity of an emergency room is 100 patients, for instance, that would be noted in the storyboard.

Adding Volume Estimates

Once each step is storyboarded, volume estimates are added to the analysis. Do customers wish to purchase 100 clay pots from your pottery studio each day? If each pot requires a half of a pound of raw clay, you'll need to find a supplier to deliver 50 pounds per day. If he can only make deliveries every 4th day, your temporary raw clay storage area needs to be large enough to hold 200 pounds of raw clay. Similar estimates must be developed for labor, equipment, and the finished goods storage area. In addition, contingency plans must be developed to address delays or problems that tend to occur in the normal course of business.

Why do all this work? Well, by performing these analyses, planners may learn that their production targets are simply unsustainable. If the treatment area of an emergency room only holds 10 beds, for instance, and if appropriate medical practices require patients to remain in that area for 2 hours prior to discharge, the hospital will only be able to discharge an average of five patients per hour regardless of the number of incoming patients, the medical staffing patterns, or any other factors. And if the severity levels of the patients require average treatment times that exceed 2 hours, a discharge rate of five patients per hour will itself be unsustainable.

Targets and Ranges

Once volume estimates are added to the storyboard, we can calculate our *most likely* volume target, one that considers all of the constraints that limit an organization's production capacity. Then we can place a range around that target, and we can list the factors that might drive volumes toward the upper or lower boundaries of that range.

Does a factory rely on deliveries of materials that arrive from a local airport? If the airport shuts down 5% of the time during normal winter months because of inclement weather, and up to 20% during times of unusually harsh weather, such statistics would help a planner project the lower boundary of the factory's volume range. On the other hand, if an alternative rail service is expected to be available up to 15% of the time—though its availability can never be guaranteed in advance— then its use might boost volume capacity toward the upper boundary of the range.

There may be hundreds, or even thousands, of small items that are utilized during a production process; does a business planner need to account for all of them? Fortunately, only items that place significant constraints on production capacity need to be noted by a planner. For example, if an emergency room can remain open even though its medical records clerk takes a day off, his presence need not be noted on the process flow analysis. But if the facility runs out of sterilization fluid, it may need to cease operations entirely until it can secure a new supply; that would certainly be a noteworthy item!

Applied Illustration

Hugh is concerned about the 24-hour e-mail response service that is operated by his agency. Although it does not receive many clinical emergency contacts—consumers usually call their physicians directly for such issues—it does receive a large number of contacts featuring questions regarding the proper use of therapeutic devices and the appropriate management of home-based exercise regimens.

Hugh has worked in the industry for many years and has witnessed the consumer communications function evolve from personal conversations to telephone interactions, and then on to e-mail correspondence. The new trend toward interactive Web sites is, quite understandably, just another transition to him.

Nevertheless, price competition is fiercer than ever. Hugh must thus ensure that his operating costs are as low as possible so he can afford to match the low fees of his deep-discount small agency competitors. Hugh's model focuses on equipping his inexperienced and low-paid e-mail response service representatives with a set of sophisticated online reference databases to help them compensate for their lack of industry knowledge.

Hugh is wondering whether he can eliminate any of his 20 service representative positions, and thus he decides to prepare a process flow analysis. Let's follow him as he prepares his analysis.

Our business model is quite simple; when a consumer contacts us by e-mail, we assign the query to a service representative who follows up by e-mail and enters the information into our system. If the question concerns a therapeutic device, our representative will consult an online database and attempt to obtain an answer to the question. If this is not possible, or if the query needs to be forwarded to the device manufacturer or to a clinician, our representative does so and then receives a response within 24 hours.

Until recently, each representative averaged 60 minutes per query, and thus we needed 20 representatives to work 40 hours weekly because our volume occasionally reached 800 queries weekly. We actually averaged 600 queries weekly, though, and at times our volume dipped to 500 queries weekly.

We are paying for an e-mail system that can handle up to 1,000 queries weekly. That's far more than we need, but the Internet service provider will only sell us broadband capacities that translate to units of 250 queries weekly. Considering our weekly boundary of 800 queries, we certainly can't make do with an e-mail capacity of only 750 . . . or can we?

A few things have changed for us recently. A small rival agency has recently withdrawn from our service area; we expect to pick up half of their consumer volume. And we expect one fourth of our volume, as well as one fourth of this new business, to come to us through interactive Web sites managed by health plans, sites that channel consumers directly to our information input screens. Those programs prompt consumers to input much of their information directly into our database before our representatives contact them; that will eventually reduce our average time per query from 60 to 20 minutes. Unfortunately, nobody understands how this is all going to work just yet, so our average time per query will actually increase to 75 minutes in the short term.

Hugh jots down the following:

- New business opportunities increase volume
- New technologies? Slows us down now, speeds us up later

Whew . . . this is a bit confusing! But hey, it's only arithmetic, so I should be able to muddle through it. Right now, we need 20 representatives to work 40 hours weekly in order to provide 800 hours of available time. And right now, our 600 queries weekly (with a range of 500 to 800) need 600 hours of service time (again, with a range of 500 to 800 hours).

That small rival is one fifth our size, which means that it was serving 120 consumers weekly (with a range of 100 to 160). If we pick up half of their volume, our consumer queries per week will increase to 660 (with a range of 550 to 880).

Now I'll consider the impact of our new Internet-based direct input system. Once our consumers and representatives learn to use it, our average query time will plummet from 60 to 20 minutes! That means that we'll only need 220 hours of representative time weekly (with a range of 183 to 293 hours) to serve the consumers, and we could get by with 500 queries of e-mail capacity. My goodness, we'd only need to employ 8 service representatives instead of 20, each working 40 hours weekly, to cover the upper boundary of our query volume range! And we could slash our e-mail capacity in half as well.

But in the short term, our average query time will increase from 60 to 75 minutes. So at the upper boundary of our range, 880 consumers would need 1,100 hours weekly of service representative time. Ouch! We'll need to increase our service staff from 20 employees to 28 to handle that volume, and we'll need to increase our e-mail capacity from 1,000 hours to 1,250 hours as well.

I suppose we'll need to increase our employee and consumer education budgets, too. That will help us drive our head count all the way down from 28 to 8 and our e-mail capacity from 1,250 to 500 as soon as possible. It's the value of education, I guess.

Hugh jots down the following:

- Higher costs now; lower costs later
- Making investments in education and training an urgent priority

Looking Forward

In this chapter, we explained how entrepreneurs can use process flow analysis to develop volume estimates for each resource utilized in the production of goods and services, as well as for each finished good or service produced. This task is important to the development of the business plan because the resource volumes serve as the foundation of all cost estimates and the finished good volumes serve as the foundation of all revenue estimates.

In the next chapter, we extend our discussion of volume estimation by exploring the issue of consumer needs. In other words, in chapter 6, we move beyond our analysis of production supply by developing an analysis of consumer demand.

CHAPTER 6

Estimating Customer Demand

About This Chapter

Chapter 6 continues our review of the volume estimation section by explaining how customer demand can be generated through the two-step process of brand recognition and purchase intention. We also describe how customer profitability analysis and new media marketing activities may be helpful in optimizing levels of demand.

Customer demand is far more difficult to estimate than production capacity because most factors that influence consumer purchase decisions lie far outside of an organization's control and influence. Nevertheless, some effort to quantify demand must be made in order to ensure that the goods and services that are produced may in fact be sold.

Estimating Customer Demand

You've convinced me that you'll be able to meet your production targets. But how can you be certain that your customers will purchase all of your goods and services? Is there anything you can do to lock in your forecasted demand, or even increase it if possible?

Have you ever noticed that certain mysterious television or print advertisements fail to clearly define their own products? Perhaps it's an image of a healthy person romping through a sun-dappled meadow, followed by a brief glimpse of the name of a new pharmaceutical drug that conveys no information about its purpose. Or perhaps it's a 10-second teaser about a new film that will be released on Memorial Day, showing nothing but the film's title and release date above a black background.

Why do firms invest huge sums of money in such advertising campaigns? In fact, how can any marketing activity be effective if the audience has no idea what is being marketed?

Brand Recognition

Organizations engage in such marketing activities because they believe that they are creating customer demand. Although classically trained economists describe demand as a function that is defined by consumers, many firms believe that they can influence and generate demand through the development and implementation of marketing messages.

These firms, though, understand that the creation of customer demand requires the successful completion of a *two-step process*. First, the target customers must recognize and be impressed by the image that is conveyed by the brand itself. This positive impression leads to the engagement of the second step, which is the sharing of product information and the decision to purchase the item.

Pharmaceutical companies and film studios invest in *brand recognition* campaigns well before their products have been fully developed and approved for sale and distribution. They do so because they know that it will be difficult to establish customer recognition if they wait too long to introduce themselves to their targets. There are so many products on the shelves and behind the counters of pharmacies, and so many commercial films released over the course of the year, that it becomes necessary to stage these brand recognition campaigns in order to remain successful.

A business plan should describe its goals and success measurements regarding its brand recognition strategy and should present cost estimates for its relevant marketing activities as well. Consumer surveys can be distributed, and focus groups can be conducted, to collect and analyze such data.

Purchase Intention

Once this first step has been completed, the sales function must then convince customers to purchase the product or service. Without brand recognition already established in the minds of the target customers, any marketing that is designed to encourage *purchase intention* will likely fall on deaf ears. Likewise, any direct selling activity regarding a brand that is unrecognized by customers will be similarly ineffective.

Pharmaceutical companies and film studios engage in purchase-intention development activities, but the format and content of their efforts are very different than what they do to ensure brand recognition. They may offer product sampling, for instance, when pharmaceutical companies distribute single-wrap pills in physician's offices, and film studios screen movie trailers in theaters. Pharmaceutical companies may also send salespeople to visit physicians in their offices, and film studios may also send movie stars to media interview events to promote their films.

As with brand recognition activities, a business plan should offer detailed descriptions, success metrics, and cost estimates for these purchase-intention activities. A planner might also consider implementing two specific options that have proven successful in many industries.

One option is known as *customer profitability analysis*. Many organizations have discovered that it is far easier, and far more profitable, to market new products and services to existing customers than to attract new customers. This phenomenon is usually attributed to the fact that the brand recognition hurdle has already been cleared with existing customers and thus requires no additional consideration.

But how should an organization identify the existing customers who should be targeted by new purchase-intention activities? The proverbial 80/20 rule often applies in such situations, meaning that only 20% of all customers should be targeted if they are generating 80% of the organization's profits. In fact, some business consultants actually recommend walking away from the bottom 20% of all customers if they represent unprofitable burdens to the enterprise.

Another option is known as *new media marketing activities*. Although the costs of placing advertisements in traditional media outlets are publicly available and highly publicized, the costs of staging new media marketing activities are far more uncertain in nature. The cost of inserting a viral marketing video on a free Internet media site, for instance, may be little or nothing, and the benefit to be derived by doing so may be enormous.

On the other hand, the cost of implementing such a plan may be equally enormous if the general public decides to ridicule a clumsily placed video on an entertainment Web site. Such contingencies are very difficult to address in a formal business plan, and yet they must be considered in order to describe a firm's comprehensive strategy for creating customer demand.

Applied Illustration

Hugh is determined to raise the public profile of his home care agency. Determined to generate consumer demand for therapeutic services in an entertaining manner, Hugh is sponsoring groups of young actors and actresses to attend community festivals and fairs this summer. They will perform brief skits about the importance of remaining physically active and in good health and will hand out freebies emblazoned with Hugh's agency logo.

Hugh says,

Hmm. The target audience is familiar with physical therapy services for severely impaired consumers, but they probably don't know that occupational therapy services can be useful for modestly impaired individuals. How can we help them realize that many of them can benefit from occupational therapy services?

He decides to launch an educational Web site that emphasizes the human needs, clinical techniques, and healthy living outcomes of occupational therapy. He also decides to place advertisements in magazines that cover summer festivals and fairs and that highlight the Web address to the site. Among various interactive activities on the site is a self-learning quiz that asks about occupational therapy in general and his agency in particular; Hugh hopes to rely on the answers of online visitors to help him measure whether he is successfully establishing brand recognition regarding the topic.

Being cautious by nature, Hugh decides to premiere his theatric performers in a few moderately sized festivals and fairs in the late spring and early summer. He decides to encourage the purchase intention of the audience by sending friendly actors and actresses in nursing uniforms to hand out "first visit free" coupons to all eligible individuals after each performance.

Hugh jots down the following:

- Brand recognition addressed via advertisements
- Purchase intention addressed via coupons
- Success metrics measured via Web site

But which festivals and fairs should be visited by Hugh's merry band of actors? Fortunately, he has access to the home address records of consumers who have attended his diner-based events during the past 5 years; he notes that 80% of all attendees live within 20% of the neighborhoods that define his agency's licensed service area. Thus, Hugh decides to target the festivals and fairs of those specific neighborhoods with his actors and actresses.

Finally, with some trepidation, he allows some of the actors to establish social networking blogs about their experiences. However, he restricts their blogging activities to a small number of Web services owned by highly reputable organizations that have established strict controls against inappropriate communications.

Hugh jots down the following:

- 80/20 rule for neighborhood festivals and fairs
- Use new media blogs to generate word of mouth

Now that Hugh has established his plans, how can he estimate the cost of these endeavors? He is fairly certain about the cost of establishing the Web site and placing advertisements in traditional media magazines because he has undertaken such activities many times in the past. He is also confident in the cost estimate that he has developed for hiring actors from a local nonprofit community theater troupe; although he has not previously launched such a campaign, he believes that its cost is quite minimal in comparison to its anticipated benefits.

He is a bit nervous, though, about the risk of permitting independent contractors to write blog entries about their experiences while working for his agency. He thus decides to purchase an insurance policy to cover any lawsuits about comments written by the actors while under contract with him. He also decides to pay a public relations firm to conduct mandatory training sessions for his actors about appropriate behaviors during promotional appearances.

The cost of the insurance premium surprises Hugh very much; after inquiring about it, he accepts the insurer's explanation that his organization possesses little prior experience in new media marketing activities and thus falls within a high-risk category. Because he strongly believes that such marketing activities may prove extremely helpful for promoting brand recognition and ultimately purchase intention, he decides to purchase the insurance policy and add the cost of its premium to the expense section of the flexible budget in his business plan.

Hugh jots down the following:

- Web site and traditional media costs easily estimated
- Cost of actor appearances easily estimated and easily justifiable
- Obtain insurance policy for blog commentary and training for appearances

Looking Forward

In this chapter, we explained how entrepreneurs can stimulate customer demand by designing programs that enhance the brand recognition and purchase-intention tendencies of consumers. This task is important to the development of the business plan because such activities are required to create the demand that will absorb the goods and services that are produced by the organization.

In the next chapter, we reconcile the concepts of production supply and consumer demand through the employment of a function called quality management. In other words, in chapter 7, we conclude the volume estimation process by reviewing the information developed in chapters 5 and 6 for the purpose of estimating the volume of goods or services that can be produced *and* sold by the organization.

CHAPTER 7

Reconciling Supply and Demand via Quality Management

About This Chapter

Chapter 7 completes our review of the volume estimation section by explaining how the techniques of quality management can be utilized to reconcile production capacity and consumer demand. We define quality management as a process that employs a mix of four activities: prevention, appraisal, internal failure, and external failure.

This chapter also addresses how quality managers should align their objectives with the short-term and long-term goals of the organization. For instance, an "always improve quality" objective may be less appropriate than a "maintain quality" objective at times when production volumes must be increased immediately, or when customers simply care less about quality than about price.

Reconciling Supply and Demand via Quality Management

Based on the previous two chapters of your plan, your customer demand is much higher than your production capacity. Obviously, you can profit by increasing capacity to meet demand, but can you maintain product quality while doing so?

It is virtually impossible to maintain production capacity at a level precisely equal to consumer demand. After all, there are usually daily fluctuations in customer requirements, and only some of them are predictable. Although an organization's own marketing activities may modify demand, factors that lie far outside of its control may cause other fluctuations.

We must therefore continually modify our production capacity to meet the ever-moving target of customer demand. But how can we anticipate movements in this target? By using customer feedback surveys, staging focus group meetings, and analyzing empirical data, we can glean the information that we need to make educated guesses about our customer's evolving needs. Then we can modify our process flow analysis to modify our output capacity.

There are times when severe recessions hit specific industries, or sometimes entire economies, necessitating dramatic *reductions* in capacity. Under normal business conditions, though, healthy companies will often need to *increase* their capacity to service the new demand that is created by their marketing activities.

The Whistle Blowers of Quality Management

Whenever production processes are modified to increase (or decrease) production, we must consider the impact of these changes on the quality of our products. After all, any change creates a risk that our quality will deteriorate until our employees understand our new system, or until our customers learn our new business practices.

In fact, when processes are modified dramatically to increase production capacity, product quality may fall into an equally dramatic nosedive. Shortcuts are often implemented to keep production processes churning away, out of concern that work stoppages may lead to unserved demand and lost sales.

Under these circumstances, quality managers often assume a very pragmatic role. Instead of advocating an "always *improve* quality" strategy, quality managers often devise practices to *maintain* current levels of quality while volume increases. In other words, when customer demand exceeds production capacity, quality managers serve as *whistle blowers* who sound alarms if quality is sacrificed to a significant extent.

The Tools of Quality Managers

So how do quality managers perform this critically important task? They tend to use four different types of activities when designing the production process.

Prevention activities are designed to eliminate any possibility that quality problems will emerge at all. Employee, supplier, and customer training programs, for instance, are prevention activities. Reference checks of employees' resumes and vendor applications are also prevention activities.

Appraisal activities are designed to detect quality problems immediately after they occur so they can be addressed quickly and effectively. Raw material, component, and assembly testing procedures, for example, are appraisal activities. Supervisors who monitor the conversations of their call center operators are performing appraisal activities as well.

Internal failure activities are response functions that are activated when prevention and appraisal activities have failed and internal crises have erupted. The shutdown of a food packaging plant to search for a contamination source is such an activity. A technician who switches a Web site to a backup server when a primary server fails is performing an internal failure activity, too.

External failure activities are also response functions, but they are activated after customers have acquired the products and are thus directly impacted by the failures. Special complaint phone numbers, warranty programs, and onsite product repair visits are all external failure activities. Public relations professionals who address embarrassing news stories about such matters perform external failure activities as well.

It's in the Mix!

Which of these four types of quality activities are most effective? Most organizations prefer to utilize all four types, with levels of reliance on each type varying by industry, firm, and situation.

Let's consider a few examples. If we purchase inexpensive bags of 20 chocolate candies and find that 1 of the 20 is inevitably misshapen because of production glitches, what are we likely to do? Most of us simply shrug and pop them all in our mouths! Thus, an ideal strategy for a candy manufacturer may involve the simple mailing of a free coupon to an occasional (and rare) angry customer. This would represent a strategy based on an *external failure activity*.

However, a firm that manufactures nuclear waste containers may need to eliminate any possibility that a defective product may reach a customer. Thus, its strategy may heavily emphasize *prevention activities*. And a casino operator may believe that it can best address the possibility of dealer theft of gambling chips by placing closed-circuit cameras in the ceiling. This would represent a strategy based on an *appraisal activity*.

In each of these examples, a collection of activities may nevertheless be implemented by the company. Candy manufacturers, for instance, do take the time to spot check their products before shipping them to market. And nuclear waste container manufacturers are indeed prepared to take action when a rare defective product reaches the finished goods stage. In other words, a reasonable mix of activities is usually implemented to maintain the quality of an organization's output.

Applied Illustration

Hugh is excited about another new business expansion opportunity. A private, for-profit independent living complex for very affluent seniors has asked him to expand a part-time clinic within their community for the exclusive use of their residents. Hugh already manages a very small clinic at this site, but high consumer demand has convinced the owners of the complex to approve an expansion of service capacity.

Hugh has thus been instructed to increase the number of treatment rooms in the clinic from four to six; however, this will pose numerous operational challenges. Hugh thinks, *The residents are a genteel bunch; they expect our clinic to be managed more like a luxury club than a health facility. The clientele won't feel comfortable if they feel cramped.*

Hugh foresees other problems as well:

We're only limiting ourselves to six rooms because the area was originally designed to hold four; even six will be a tight fit. And with all of these new consumers arriving for services, we might run out of treatment rooms at the busiest times of the day. The affluent clientele will simply refuse to wait for care for any significant amount of time.

In other words, Hugh understands that the quality of the service lies in the clientele's level of satisfaction with the entire experience and not simply with the effectiveness of the therapists. Thus, by ramping up service capacity by only two rooms (which may be insufficient) and thus risking "waiting for care" situations, Hugh is concerned that the quality of his client's experience might be decimated.

Hugh jots down the following:

- Continuing undersupply of treatment rooms may lead to a catastrophic cost of failure

How does Hugh plan to address this situation? He decides to focus on *prevention activities* and, to a lesser extent (as a backup function), on *appraisal activities* as well. He muses,

If we fail to immediately treat a single person who arrives with an expectation of immediate service, our reputation will blow up in our faces. This community is a small and closed social environment; just one miffed consumer can spread his dissatisfaction around the clientele like a rampant virus. It can destroy our demand for services throughout the entire complex . . . and perhaps spread to similar senior living complexes as well.

So that means we'll need to require our clientele to make advance reservations for treatment rooms; one of us should pick up each phone call on the first ring so that no one is left waiting. We must also find a way to justify our new reservations policy in the name of consumer satisfaction, but how can we do that?

Hey, I have an idea! We can promise our clientele that their favorite healthy snack and energy drink will be waiting for them, perfectly chilled, when they arrive. Of course, a waiter from the private club restaurant next door will come by immediately after each consumer's arrival to ensure that the food is satisfactory, thereby performing a backup appraisal activity. If all progresses according to plan, though, the waiter will simply be told that everything is fine. And the consumers will need at least 15 or 20 minutes to consume their snacks before progressing into the treatment rooms, thereby giving us a little time to ensure that the rooms are available for them.

Hugh jots down the following:

- Snack order used as rationale for reservation requirement
- Reservation system *prevents* "waiting for care" situations
- Rely on waiters to perform *appraisal* activity

But this is going to complicate our process flow analysis considerably. I'll need to inform our administrative staff that they might see a surge of calls coming to us at peak times, and that our consumers cannot experience busy signals. We might also need to equip our therapists with mobile phones and have them take reservations when our administrators and I are fully occupied and cannot take calls.

Then there is the matter of the private club restaurant next door. We use their waiters and kitchen staff to prepare and deliver our snack orders; we treat them as members of our team. I'll need to advise them that our arrival orders must be expedited ahead of any other orders, even those that are placed by their own restaurant guests. If we promise our consumers that a snack will be waiting for them upon arrival, we had better deliver it without exception.

We might need to request new budget outlays for training expenses and to increase our staffing levels as well. My administrative manager and I may also need to upgrade our technology. But, hey . . . if we're doing this to accommodate a large number of new consumers, there should be new revenue to cover these new expenses.

I guess I need to go back and change many of the numbers in my flexible budget; perhaps I should also rethink my process chain as well. If I must start pleasing my consumers the moment they call for a treatment room, well before they arrive to receive care, I'll be using a very different business model!

Hugh jots down the following:

- Rethink flexible budget assumptions
- Transformation of our process chain

Looking Forward

In this chapter, we concluded our review of volume estimation by utilizing techniques of quality management to reconcile supply and demand. This task is important to the development of the business plan because the establishment of a reliable sales volume estimate is a fundamental preliminary step to estimating costs and revenues and thus to establishing the profitability of an organization.

In the next chapter, we proceed to the cost estimation section of the business plan by analyzing the direct and indirect costs of producing our goods and services. In other words, in chapter 8, we use the information developed in our process flow analysis in chapter 5—after it has been reconciled to our customer demand analysis in chapters 6 and 7—to develop a comprehensive understanding of the cost structure of our enterprise.

PART IV

Cost Estimation

CHAPTER 8

Estimating Direct and Indirect Costs

About This Chapter

Chapter 8 begins our review of the cost estimation section by explaining how profitability should be assessed through the quantification of direct and indirect costs. Direct costs are expenditures that are required to produce and distribute goods and services, whereas indirect costs are expenditures that are required to maintain the organizational infrastructure and for other purposes.

The estimation of direct costs, in particular, is complicated by the need to match sales revenue with the costs that are required to produce them. For instance, if a cost expenditure must be made today to produce a good or service that will be sold tomorrow, it needs to be included in tomorrow's statement of income or profit and not in today's statement.

Estimating Direct and Indirect Costs

The volume numbers that you developed for your process flow analysis are pretty reasonable; now it's time to develop cost estimates for it as well. And speaking of costs, they won't exceed your revenues, will they?

Prior to the dawn of the industrial age, manufacturers didn't use assembly lines to build their products. Instead, artisans sat at benches and created each finished good from start to finish. That approach helped manufacturers design some uniquely beautiful products, but without mass production techniques, they were unable to achieve economies of scale and maintain low costs.

Amazingly, some service industries still appear to operate in a preindustrial manner. College professors, for instance, appear to teach entire courses from start to finish by themselves.

Or do they? In a sense, they don't do that at all. Most instructors outsource their reading assignments to textbook publishers. And they rely on graduate assistants to supervise lab work and grade papers. Furthermore, when they do schedule office hours to meet with students, they tend to stockpile them and then schedule them shortly before examination time, when the demand for their time is at a maximum.

Thus, even college courses have *pipelines* of predefined events that require materials (e.g., textbooks and the students who read them), labor (e.g., instructors and graduate assistants), overhead (e.g., the classroom itself), and other costs that are deferred or carried forward from period to period (e.g., office hour time stockpiled for subsequent use). In fact, any business can *storyboard* its activities in pipeline format, and any business can *cost out* its storyboard using cost analysis techniques.

Asking Five Questions

The fundamentals of direct and indirect costing are actually quite simple. We begin by asking five questions, each one building upon the previous one, as we move from a narrow focus to a broad perspective. By answering all five questions, we can prove that we are prepared to manage our operations in a cost-efficient manner.

Here are our five questions, listed in the order that we address them:

1. *What is the cost of all of the material that we directly use to produce our goods and services each day?* If we purchase more material than we need, we waste money. But if we purchase less, we won't survive until the end of the day.
2. *What is the cost of all of the resources that we directly use to produce our goods and services each day?* Once we answer question 1 regarding our direct material supply, we must do the same for our direct labor supply and our direct overhead items as well. When we refer to direct overhead, we mean any direct resource (other than direct material and direct labor) that is required to produce our goods and services.

3. *What is the cost of the resources that we directly use to produce "completed goods and services" each day?* How often do we experience days when we burn through our time and resources and accomplish nothing? Whereas questions 1 and 2 address the value of the resources that we are using (i.e., burning), question 3 addresses the value of the goods and services that we are completing and preparing for sale.

4. *What is the total direct cost of the "completed goods and services" that we sell each day?* How often do we experience days when we complete many tasks, but none of them is marketable? Whereas question 3 addresses the value of the goods and services that we are completing and preparing for sale each day, question 4 addresses the value of the goods and services that we actually sell each day.

Is it possible for a service to be completed one day but not sold until the next day? You bet! If a landscaper completes a lawn-seeding service today, but cannot consider the project closed and sold until the home proprietor inspects his work tomorrow, a management accounting system would classify it as completed today and sold tomorrow.

5. *What do we earn each day, net of all indirect costs?* At the end of each day, we must ensure that we will generate sufficient revenues to (a) cover the direct costs of producing the goods and services that are sold, (b) cover the indirect costs of any other relevant business expenses, and (c) generate a reasonable level of profits.

Of course, we don't necessarily need to choose a day as our unit of time; instead, we can choose any period that is meaningful to us. Movie studios, for instance, track results on a weekly basis because movie "grosses" are announced in that manner. And landlords of residential properties employ a monthly basis because lease payments are often required in that time frame.

A Little Arithmetic

Now we must use a little arithmetic to answer our five questions. Let's begin by defining our terms:

Our stockpiles of direct material are our deferred *direct material* (DM) costs. Our stockpiles of completed items are our deferred *finished goods and services* (FG) costs. And the volumes of work that are advancing through our system at any given time are our deferred *work in process* (WIP) costs.

Aren't we referring to inventories when we refer to DM, WIP, and FG? Yes, but these items may refer to other types of deferred costs as well. For instance, a software engineering firm may need to defer direct labor costs into WIP and FG for service contracts that are in process but not yet completed. And if a school prepurchases a fixed number of logins to access an online database, it may need to account for these prepaid activities as deferred DM.

In addition, our purchases (P) is the money we spend to acquire our DM. Our direct labor (DL) is what we spend to pay our direct service employees. Our overhead (OH) is what we spend for all other direct resources that are required to produce our goods and services. And our indirect expenditures (IE) are what we spend for all nonproduction activities.

What do we do with these terms? We use them to create five simple arithmetic formulas, each one designed to answer one of our questions:

1. *Cost of DM Used = DM @ Start of Day + P − DM @ End of Day.* We begin the day by using any material that is already in storage. Then we use whatever we purchase today, except for any portion of our purchases that we store until tomorrow.
2. *Cost of All Resources Used = DM Used From Question 1 + DL Used + OH Used.* In addition to accounting for the direct materials that we use today, we also must account for the direct labor and other direct resources as well.
3. *Cost of Goods and Services Completed = WIP @ Start of Day + Resources Used From Question 2 − WIP @ End of Day.* Some of the goods and services that we complete today were started yesterday, and thus we include them by beginning with WIP @ Start of Day. And some of the resources that we use today will remain in WIP @ End of Day; they will be included in tomorrow's Cost of Goods and Services Completed.

In other words, we begin today by completing whatever goods and services were started yesterday. Then we continue completing whatever we are working on today, except for the portion of today's work that we store until tomorrow.

4. *Cost of Goods and Services Sold = FG @ Start of Day + Cost of Goods and Services Completed From Question 3 – FG @ End of Day.* This formula is similar to formulas 1 and 3. We begin the day by selling whatever goods and services were completed and stockpiled yesterday. Then we sell whatever we complete today, except for the portion that we store until tomorrow.

5. *Revenue—Cost of Goods and Services Sold From Question 4 – IE = Earnings.* Our earnings are simply the difference between our revenues and our various costs.

Applied Illustration

Every morning, Hugh checks the direct costing profitability reports of his home-based nursing service for accident victims. Health plans only pay fixed lump sum amounts for care once consumers achieve certain clinical outcomes (such as, for instance, the ability to walk in an unaided manner), and he is concerned that his nurses are requiring too many visits to achieve these goals.

Hugh prepares a direct costing schedule on a daily basis; he knows that he must encourage his nurses to expedite their care plans because of an imminent increase in new referrals. Thus, direct material and work-in-progress cost deferrals will increase as well.

As always, Hugh arrives at 7:00 a.m. to review these reports and confirm that his staff is ready to begin operations. His two home care nurses arrive at 8:00 a.m. and then immediately head out for their first cases; they each work 7.5 hours.

This morning, Hugh says,

I'm starting the day with DM of $2,000; those are the bandages, over-the-counter medications, and other items that my nurses use with consumers. I have already expended $50,000 of direct costs for my roster of cases in process; that is my WIP. And I have expended $1,000 on *a brief case that has already been completed but that is awaiting the health plan's final chart review; that is my FG ready for sale.*

I've already ordered another $10,000 of DM to be delivered today, and I'm paying my workers $2,000 for DL. My OH will total $2,000 and my IE will total $100.

The health plans usually pay me fees at a price of 10% over my direct costs; I'm hoping to complete and "sell" (meaning to walk the health plans through a completion of their chart review process) $3,000 (premarkup) or more of FG to them today. Because I need to encourage my nurses to prepare for an imminent increase in new referrals, I'd prefer to end today with 20% more DM, WIP, and FG than when I begin today. Is this all possible?

Hugh takes a deep breath and starts plugging numbers into his formulas. Here are his calculations:

DM Used = $2,000 + $10,000 − $2,400 = $9,600.

All Resources Used = $9,600 + $2,000 + $2,000 = $13,600.

Goods and Services Completed = $50,000 + $13,600 − $60,000 = $3,600.

Goods and Services Sold = $1,000 + $3,600 − $1,200 = $3,400.

Earnings = $3,740 − $3,400 − $100 = $240.

Hugh jots down the following:

- Meeting DM, WIP, and FG targets
- Positive earnings

This looks reasonable. But Hugh, being cautious by nature, runs a few *control checks* to ensure that these plans are achievable. He asks himself,

Are my cost of goods and services sold greater than my $3,000 target? Yes, they're equal to $3,400 . . . check! Are $240 in earnings sufficient? Well, $240 per day equals $1,680 per week or $87,360 per year. I pay myself dividends of $6,000 per month from this accident victim service, so I only need to generate $72,000 of earnings per year. Once again . . . check!

Well, I'm glad that I used these five formulas to check my numbers. Now I should skim my quality management notes to see whether we can hasten production even further to increase our output without harming the quality of our products.

Hugh jots down the following:

- Control checks all positive
- Might be able to push harder; review quality notes

Looking Forward

In this chapter, we began our review of cost estimation by utilizing techniques of direct and indirect costing to develop a preliminary assessment of profitability. This task is important to the development of the business plan because we need to match the deferred costs of DM, WIP, and FG to the periods when the goods and services that they produce will be generating revenues.

In the next chapter, we proceed to the activity-based costing section of the business plan by "costing" out organizational costs on a product-by-product or service-by-service basis. In other words, in chapter 9, we ascertain whether certain goods and services may be generating losses (or otherwise dragging down profits) even though the organization as a whole is profitable.

CHAPTER 9

Assessing Cost Structures With Activity-Based Costing

About This Chapter

Chapter 9 continues our review of the cost estimation section by explaining how the cost structures of different product and service lines can be analyzed through activity-based costing. Organizations must define activities for each product or service, assign cost drivers to each activity, and then allocate costs to each activity in proportion to the fluctuations of the cost drivers.

There are a variety of strategic decisions that may be undertaken by an organization if an activity-based costing analysis reveals that the cost of producing a product or service is relatively high. The firm might decide to raise its price if consumers are willing to pay a premium amount. Or it might decide to search for approaches to reduce its direct costs of production. Alternatively, it may simply decide to absorb the losses for strategic reasons, although (in this scenario) it might feel compelled to maintain relatively small volumes in order to minimize losses.

Assessing Cost Structures With Activity-Based Costing

You've convinced me that your cost estimates are reasonable, and that your overall business concept can be profitable. But I'm concerned that you might not be focusing on your most efficient business opportunities. Aren't some of your products more expensive to produce than others?

Are you familiar with a concept called the *80/20 rule?* We mentioned it earlier in chapter 6; it's all about focusing on your most profitable opportunities. According to the rule, 80% of an organization's profits are often generated by only 20% of its products or customers.

In such situations, the easiest way to improve profitability in percentage terms is to simply eliminate 80% of one's business. Profits may drop 20%, but the elimination of so much dead weight can liberate a tremendous array of organizational resources to pursue more promising business prospects.

Not all organizations face 80/20 situations, of course, but most firms can indeed increase profit percentages significantly by simply pruning relatively unprofitable products or customers from their books. But how can they determine whether any given item is relatively profitable or unprofitable?

This is the purpose of *activity-based costing* (ABC). Some organizations actually do use ABC to identify customer relationships that should be terminated. Nevertheless, although some organizations consider this strategy to be rather extreme, they often prepare ABC analyses and then use the data to demand price increases from their costliest customers.

Activities and Cost Drivers

ABC is an accounting analysis that is produced by a system known as *activity-based management* (ABM). At a fundamental level, ABM requires managers to break down their systems of production into sequences of individual activities.

The storyboarding process can provide a helpful starting point for preparing ABM and ABC analyses, though additional details must be added to its descriptions of process flow in order to utilize it effectively. For instance, if three different individuals work together to assemble a floral arrangement in a retail gift shop, the *final assembly* stage might be represented by a *single* descriptive item in the storyboard. However, if one person snips the bottom of each flower, a second person inserts each flower into a vase, and a third person adds a handful of plant food packets, *each of the three* tasks might be represented by its own descriptive item in an ABM analysis.

We also need to define a *cost driver* for each activity, a name that was coined because it refers to the measurable functions that *drive* costs higher. The cost driver of a factory's lighting and heating activity, for instance, might be the square footage of each production area because the size of an area *drives* (i.e., determines) the cost of making it habitable. But the cost of maintaining a factory machine that must be operated one time for each item produced might be the number of items that are produced each day.

Cost Allocations

With activities and cost drivers in hand, we may proceed to estimate the cost of any item that is produced by an organization or the cost of any customer that is served by it. To perform this task, we simply list all of the activities that must be performed in order to create an item or serve a customer, then we use our cost driver data to allocate our costs. For instance, does it cost $100 per minute to heat a room that is used to manufacture nuts and bolts? Is the floor space of the room dedicated 75% to nut production and 25% to bolt production? Furthermore, does it cost another $100 per minute to operate a machine that is employed once for each nut and once for each bolt? Based on this information, if we produce 10 nuts and 10 bolts each minute, it would cost $125 to produce 10 nuts and $75 to produce 10 bolts. In other words, each nut would cost $12.50 and each bolt would cost $7.50; the firm might thus consider dropping its nut customers if they are unwilling to pay higher prices than bolt customers.

Some organizations mistakenly believe that ABC is not relevant to them because they only produce a single product. Nevertheless, they often need to dedicate different amounts of administrative resources to different categories of customers. For example, although airlines refer to their *Internet only* fares as *special discount* prices, they actually charge *premium* prices to customers who insist on booking their tickets by telephone. Although Internet and telephone customers each purchase an identical service, telephone customers are actually much more costly to serve than Internet customers from an indirect administrative perspective.

Applied Illustration

Hugh is concerned about a clinical management contract that his maternity nurses maintain with a major metropolitan hospital. Under the management of Hugh's home care clinicians, the institution has become embroiled in a series of angry disputes with several health insurance companies about the efficiency of its maternity services; it is now attempting to address their concerns by establishing more cost effective clinical practices and then sharing the savings by lowering its charges (i.e., its prices).

Apparently, due to the lack of prenatal education services and the existence of numerous environmental stressors in the local residential community, the hospital has experienced a dramatic increase in the number of false labor admissions. Insurers argue that such admissions are not medically necessary and thus should not be billed to them, but Hugh's clinical management team asserts that any pregnant woman who is approaching her delivery date must be admitted immediately if she presents herself to the institution.

As a compromise solution, the hospital and Hugh's agency have agreed to establish a clinical observation area that can serve as a portal to the maternity ward (for women who are truly going into labor) or to an expedited discharge (for women who are experiencing false labor). Hugh has been asked to estimate the costs to provide care to each type of patient for purposes of establishing a dual-rate charge (i.e., price) structure.

Hugh muses,

First, I'll review our storyboard to see how we've broken down this process. Hmm. Basically, each woman spends a little time in the new observation area and undergoes our admission screening process there. Then each woman spends a day in the hospital, with each false labor patient undergoing a battery of medical tests to ensure that her unborn child is healthy and with each successful delivery patient leading to a maternity stay for mother and baby. Finally, all three types of patients—the false labor women, the new mothers, and the babies— undergo a screening and education process prior to discharge.

Hugh jots down the following:

- Observation area serves as a portal
- Storyboard: observation to testing (or delivery) to discharge

Hugh starts to list every activity that each type of patient undergoes in the hospital; he begins to feel overwhelmed by the process. But then a flash of inspiration hits him.

Wait a minute! I don't really need to list all of the items, just the differential items. The goal of this task is to establish differential rates between false labor cases and new birth cases, so when women in both categories undergo the same activities, the discount that we apply to false labor cases won't be affected by them.

Feeling more confident about his assignment, Hugh proceeds to break down his storyboard functions into detailed lists of activities. He says,

> On average, 200 women enter the hospital each month claiming to be in labor. Half of them proceed to give birth to babies, but half of them are unknowingly experiencing false labor pains. Wow! No wonder the health insurers are frustrated by our track record.
>
> What's next? Well, I suppose I should get my activities and cost drivers in order. Prior to admission, each patient represents a case to us, and we've always said that the number of cases drives our costs. But after admission, each mother who gives birth adds a second patient (i.e., a baby) to her case. From that point forward, I need to remember that the number of patients each day drives our costs, not the number of cases.

Hugh jots down the following:

- Before delivery, 1 case = 1 patient
- After delivery, 1 case = 2 patients, but *not* for false labor patients

> Now, what about our differential activities? Well, we spend an equal amount of resources on each case that enters our new observation area. So, for the cases that result in births, I guess we should split the predelivery costs between the women and their babies.
>
> Also, for each false labor case, the hospital brings in an obstetrician prior to discharge to perform a series of follow-up medical tests. We obviously don't need to do that for mothers who deliver babies.
>
> Finally, each patient (i.e., each woman and each baby) is placed through a series of administrative discharge activities. During this time, we spend a lot of time on paperwork, with babies requiring twice as much administrative effort as adults because of our need to register them as citizens with the appropriate authorities.
>
> And how much money do we expend on these functions? According to our fiscal controller, we spend about $100k in total for each function per month. In other words, we spend $100k for the observation work, $100k for the obstetrician, and $100k for the administrative paperwork.

Hugh thus creates the following table (see Table 9.1).

Table 9.1.

	False labor	Mother	Baby	Total
Observation	$50	$25	$25	$100
Obstetrician	$100	$0	$0	$100
Paperwork	$25	$25	$50	$100
Total	$175	$50	$75	$300

Hugh exclaims,

Now this is interesting! I never would have realized this if I hadn't prepared this analysis. False labor patients are actually far more expensive than the other patients; they cost more than mothers and their babies combined. And it's primarily due to the obstetrics work.

Hmm. I suppose that the hospital might be able to spin that off into a freestanding ambulatory service center, in the manner that we created our new maternity observation center. It wouldn't bring down the overall costs of care, but by charging for the obstetrics work under a separate contract, our maternity prices might become more marketable to insurers.

Hugh jots down the following:

- False labor justifies premium prices, not discounts
- Consider spinoff of obstetrics function

Looking Forward

In this chapter, we continued our review of cost estimation by utilizing a technique of activity-based management called activity-based costing. This task is important to the development of the business plan because an organization must understand which of its goods and services are generating the highest costs, thereby draining the profits of the organization.

In the next chapter, we conclude the cost estimation section of the business plan by employing variance analysis to assess our ability to maintain our cost structure. In other words, in chapter 10, we ascertain whether we are prepared to manage situations where actual costs are significantly different than the budgeted levels that appear in our business plan.

CHAPTER 10

Risk Management With Cost Variance Analysis

About This Chapter

Chapter 10 completes our review of the cost estimation section by explaining how the cost structure of the organization can be assessed through variance analysis. This topic serves as a preliminary example of the field of risk management, a discipline that is addressed in far more detail throughout part VII of this book.

The purpose of cost variance analysis is to identify the underlying reason(s) why actual costs vary from budgeted or planned amounts. For instance, quantity component variances occur when quantities actually purchased are not equal to quantities planned for purchase. Likewise, price component variances occur when unit prices actually paid for purchase are not equal to unit prices planned for purchase.

Risk Management With Cost Variance Analysis

Your cost structure looks good in theory, but theory often fails to hold up under the stresses of reality. You might experience all sorts of cost overruns—prices hikes, supply spoilage, that sort of thing. Do you know how you'd handle those types of problems?

Wouldn't it be nice if our plans always worked out in reality? There would be no need to track actual results; we could simply use our plans to compile our financial statements, file our tax returns, and prepare our subsequent set of plans for the following year.

Unfortunately, life doesn't work out that way, in our personal lives or in our professional lives. In fact, the world has become such an uncertain place that we often need to update our plans on the fly by comparing them to our actual results on an ongoing basis.

But what do we do when our results are not consistent with our original plans? Although there may be times when such fluctuations are caused by completely unforeseeable and unmanageable events, it is more often true that someone is to blame when such variances occur. Sometimes it is the fault of a budgeter for preparing a plan that was fundamentally unrealistic and unachievable in nature. And sometimes it is the fault of a manager for failing to execute a reasonable plan.

Whenever such variances are significant, senior managers must bluntly ask, "Is someone at fault here? Whom shall we blame? And, if necessary, whom shall we fire?" The purpose of variance analysis is to provide the data that answer these questions.

Breaking Down Totals Into Components

We begin any variance analysis by quantifying the difference between an original *budget* amount and a subsequent *actual* amount. The budget amount is sometimes called the *standard* balance, and the actual amount is sometimes called the *real* balance. The process is quite simple; the total variance is calculated as the difference between these two amounts or balances.

For instance, if we originally expect to spend $10 million, and we eventually end up spending $12 million, we experience a $2 million variance in an *unfavorable* direction. On the other hand, if we only end up spending $9 million, we experience a $1 million variance in a *favorable* direction.

We then break down this *total* variance into its component details. Is any part of our supply cost variance caused by the fact that the price we actually pay is different than the price that we predicted while preparing our original budget? Then the portion of the total variance that is attributable to this difference would be called our *rate component* variance.

Alternatively, is any part of our supply cost variance caused by the fact that the amount of supplies that we actually buy is different than the amount that we initially predicted? Then the portion of the total variance attributable to this difference would be called our *quantity component* variance.

Any other underlying reason for a difference between the actual cost and the budgeted cost would also be represented by a component variance. Of course, the sum of the component variances must always equal the total; it never hurts to check that total for arithmetic accuracy.

Investigating the Reasons

After completing these calculations, we must investigate each component variance and ask ourselves why it was formed—in other words, whom should be blamed for its existence. For instance, does an unfavorable price variance exist because the price that we are paying for supplies exceeds the predicted price in our original budget? That might be the fault of the manager who actually negotiated a foolishly high price, or it might be the fault of the budget analyst who originally established an unrealistically low price target.

How about a favorable quantity variance that exists because the amount of supplies that we are consuming this year is much less than the amount originally budgeted? Don't be so fast to congratulate your supplies manager; before you do so, check first to see whether the original budget was a realistic one.

The most complicated analyses are the ones encompassing several component variances that are simultaneously in play and that are not all pointing in the same direction. Some may be favorable and some may be unfavorable, making it necessary for managers to differentiate between employees who deserve to be rewarded and those who deserve to be punished.

Applied Illustration

Hugh is in a panic about his agency's gasoline costs. Although he once simply reimbursed his home care nurses for their retail gasoline purchases, he realized some time ago that he could recognize significant savings by purchasing fuel in wholesale markets by the gallon and then requiring his nurses to "gas up" every morning at a pump within his office complex.

Hugh recently flew into a rage when he learned that his agency overspent its fuel budget by an enormous $1.25 million last year. He decided to prepare a variance analysis and quantify, as he phrased it, "the number of people whom I need to fire to ensure that this never happens again."

Hugh sits down, laughs nervously, and prepares to begin his analytical task. He thinks,

> *First, I should confirm that we really did go over budget by $1.25 million last year. Hmm . . . we originally planned to spend $10 million, and we actually spent $11.25 million. Yep, we're $1.25 million in the hole. No wonder I feel so upset!*
>
> *Now I'm ready to drill down into the details. We originally planned to buy 200,000 gallons of fuel at $50 per gallon; that's why we budgeted $10 million. But we actually purchased 250,000 gallons of fuel at $45 per gallon; that multiplies out to $11.25 million. Well, I guess we have two component variances here, a price variance and a rate variance.*

Hugh jots down the following:

- Total variance is negative
- At first glance, two component variances

Hugh then begins to conduct an investigation of these two variances. However, after speaking to several colleagues, he starts to realize that the situation is a bit more complicated than he originally suspected. He muses,

> *I first assumed that we mistakenly overshot our purchase quantity budget by 50,000 gallons, but that's a misleading number. What really happened is a series of different events that happened to produce that 50,000 gallon difference.*
>
> *At first, our transportation fleet manager told our gasoline market buyer that driving activity would be "way up" this quarter; thus, he asked our buyer to increase our normal purchase volume. The buyer then raised his purchase orders from 200,000 to 250,000 gallons. But our schedulers simultaneously implemented some revisions in the way that we assign cases to nurses, giving each nurse a "local zone" that reduced driving time. That held usage down to 220,000*

gallons, so even though we bought 250,000 gallons, we only used 220,000 gallons.

Wow, this is getting complicated, so let me backtrack and calculate the component variances before I start assessing blame. The $5 reduction in our price per gallon saved us $1.25 million across the 250,000 gallons that we purchased; that's a $1.25 million favorable variance. The difference between the original 200,000 gallon total in our budget and the 220,000 gallons that we actually used, valued at $50 per gallon, is a $1.0 million unfavorable variance. And the difference between the 220,000 gallons that we actually used and the 250,000 that we purchased, valued at $50 per gallon, is a $1.5 million unfavorable variance.

Before I continue, let me confirm that my component variances add up to my total. A favorable $1.25 million plus an unfavorable $1.5 million plus an unfavorable $1.0 million equals an unfavorable $1.25 million . . . and $1.25 million is my total variance! So my arithmetic is correct, and now I can proceed to assess blame.

Hugh jots down the following:

- One favorable rate component variance
- Two unfavorable quantity component variances

I always prefer to assess the bad news before the good news, so let me address the unfavorable variances first. My guess is that the budget analyst who originally predicted that we'd use 200,000 gallons didn't bother to reach out to the transportation manager for a reliable estimate, so I'm blaming that budget analyst for our $1 million unfavorable component variance.

The $1.5 million unfavorable component variance is a tougher one to assess. Our market buyer insists that our transportation manager only told him to increase his purchases "way up," and that he was justified in buying 250,000 gallons of fuel. But the transportation manager insists that he said "up by 10%" and not "way up," and thus he refuses to accept blame for any purchase amounts beyond 220,000 gallons. My guess is that they're both to blame for bad communication practices, but I'll take a little more time to mull over that one.

Of course, our $1.25 million total variance would be twice as bad if not for a smart young guy in our Purchasing Department who asked, "If we're increasing our purchase volume from 200,000 to 250,000 gallons, why don't we ask for a purchase discount?" Though that guy may only be a part-time intern working his way through college, he saved us $1.25 million! I would never have known about him if not for my variance analysis work; I want to make sure that the young man is clearly recognized and amply rewarded.

Hugh jots down the following:

- Budget analyst at fault for $1 million variance
- Transport manager and market buyer share blame for $1.5 million variance
- Part-time intern should be rewarded for $1.25 million variance

Looking Forward

In this chapter, we concluded our review of cost estimation by utilizing a risk management technique called variance analysis to assess differences between actual and budgeted costs. This task is important to the development of the business plan because these two cost amounts often vary to a significant extent; thus, an organization's financial health is dependent upon its ability to understand the source of these fluctuations, and to assess blame accordingly.

In the next chapter, we begin the revenue estimation section of the business plan by utilizing distinctions between fixed costs and variable costs to make price targeting decisions. In other words, in chapter 11, we utilize the volume data developed in part III and the cost data developed in part IV to make the pricing decisions that determine our revenues.

PART V

Revenue Estimation

CHAPTER 11

Price Targeting on the Basis of Cost Behavior

About This Chapter

Chapter 11 begins our review of the revenue estimation section by explaining how our knowledge of our organization's cost behavior affects our pricing decisions and thus our profitability. By differentiating between costs that remain fixed across different volume levels and costs that vary across different volume levels, we can estimate the target (i.e., planned or budgeted) price that would be required to earn any specific level of profit.

Thus, in this chapter, we establish an analytical process that emphasizes a self-focused consideration of an organization's internal cost structure. Chapters 12 and 13 then expand this self-focused analytical process to encompass more complex considerations that involve the pricing decisions of competitor organizations.

Price Targeting on the Basis of Cost Behavior

Okay, you've convinced me that your cost estimates are solid. But what about your revenue estimates? I need to know whether your target prices are going to cover your costs and produce a profit that is large enough to make this endeavor worthwhile.

Let's take a moment and review our progress. By the time that we reach this section of the business plan, we have already completed a comprehensive assessment of our business model, an analysis of the volume that we will produce and sell to our customers, and an estimation of the costs that we will incur by doing so. The next logical step, beginning with this chapter, is to assess our plans to generate the revenue that will cover these costs and produce the profits to be reinvested in new opportunities for growth.

Whew! That's a mighty long sentence, isn't it? Let's restate it in a more colloquial manner: We now must ensure that we can obtain the fuel we need to feed our production machine.

Some people are uncomfortable with the conceptualization of their business processes as machinery. In fact, some complain that such references demean their employees, whom they call "partners" or "associates" instead of "labor." We assure such individuals that our conceptualization does not conflict with their desire to nurture and celebrate human inspiration. It simply focuses on the truism that the level of efficiency of any process can always be enhanced by breaking it down into components and examining each item, just as an automobile engineer works at deconstructing an engine.

Other people are uncomfortable with the assumption that a target profit level is appropriate. Such individuals often work for nonprofit or governmental entities, where the target profit may be zero because they are obligated to return any surpluses of revenues over costs to their sources of capital. Others may work for start-up businesses that intend to produce a loss in the short term in order to establish their competitive business positions.

We assure such individuals that our profit assumption is consistent with their organizational priorities. Such entities do indeed target a specific level of profit, be it zero or negative in nature, and thus do need to produce sufficient revenues to hit their targets squarely.

Cost Behavior

"Wait a minute!" some business planners may now exclaim at this revenue section of our process. "Why didn't we list our variable and fixed costs in the cost section of our plan? How could we have proceeded to this revenue section without doing so? Aren't variable and fixed costs important?"

Yes, of course they are important. But they aren't needed to estimate costs in total; we've already accomplished that task in our previous section. Those concepts are helpful, though, in helping us understand how our cost structure *behaves* over time, which will help us determine whether our revenue will be sufficient to cover them in the future.

Variable and Fixed Costs

A *variable cost* is something that forces us to incur a cost every time we produce and sell another item. The coffee beans that are used by a snack shop to produce each cup, for instance, are variable costs. The paper coffee cups, in fact, are variable costs as well.

A *fixed cost* is something that forces us to incur a flat charge whenever we open for business, whether or not we produce and sell a single item. The monthly rental payments for a snack shop's locations, for instance, are fixed costs. The annual fees for their business licenses are fixed costs as well.

How Does It Work? Why Does It Matter?

So how do these costs *behave* over time? Fortunately for us, they behave in a very predictable manner. Variable costs vary *in total* as volume increases, but their *per-unit* costs stay fixed, at least in the short term. And fixed costs stay fixed *in total* as volume increases, but their *per-unit* costs actually decline . . . again, at least in the short term.

Shall we review an example of these behaviors? If our snack shop spends 50 cents in *variable* costs to produce each cup of coffee, that number will remain *fixed* in place until we achieve a sufficiently high volume level to earn a vendor discount. And if we pay $2,000 in fixed rental costs when we sell 2,000 cups of coffee, our *fixed* cost per unit will *drop* below $1 once we sell our 2,001st cup.

But why should we care? How does this distinction between fixed and variable costs help us manage our business? With the use of a handy little arithmetic formula, one that we'll introduce in the following applied illustration, we can use this distinction to determine whether our target price is sufficient to meet our needs.

Applied Illustration

Hugh's attention has now turned to a small but profitable ancillary government service contract called Food2U. Financed by the state government's Office for Geriatric Services of the Department of Health, the contract requires Hugh to deliver nutritious meals to geriatric consumers who spend their days at senior centers throughout the region. Although there are no clinical services directly financed by the contract, Hugh is permitted to place small promotional items within each meal box, making it an attractive business proposition for his agency.

Because Hugh's consumers have various dietary restrictions and needs, Food2U must provide a variety of meals with differing cost structures. Hugh's most popular meal, though, is his least expensive product, a small turkey roll and fruit box that contains relatively few calories and can remain unrefrigerated for long periods of time.

Hugh's Food2U line is highly profitable because Hugh charges the state $3.50 for each meal and then subcontracts all orders to small independent vendors. In other words, Hugh contracts with "mom and pop" catering firms to prepare and deliver the boxes at a total cost of $2.50 per box. Under complex state cost reporting laws, Hugh is also permitted to charge a fixed total of $45,000 in agency administrative costs against the contract.

Ordinarily, any net surpluses earned by the agency on this contract must be returned to the state at the end of the year. A prestigious research foundation, though, has recently announced a public/private partnership with the Department of Health, one that allows agencies to reinvest net surpluses in program growth opportunities if they qualify for quality improvement (QI) grant funds from the foundation. But there is a catch; the QI grant program features a restrictive minimum funding amount of $100,000. Because net surplus reinvestments must "match" all grant funds on a one-to-one basis, Hugh must find a way to generate $100,000 or more in profits from Food2U in order to keep his net surpluses and earn the matching grant funds as well.

Food2U has never managed to achieve this profit target, but Hugh suspects that a relatively modest price surcharge to be paid by the senior centers might help it do so. Hugh can't remember a handy little arithmetic

Table 11.1.

	100,000 meals	145,000 meals	200,000 meals
Revenue @ $3.50	350,000	507,500	700,000
Variable costs @ $2.50	250,000	362,500	500,000
Subtotal	100,000	145,000	200,000
Fixed costs	45,000	45,000	45,000
Net surplus to be reinvested in program growth	55,000	100,000	155,000

formula that he learned from his business planning book, so he decides to develop a spreadsheet to estimate profits across a reasonable range of volumes and prices. He begins by creating the three columns in Table 11.1

Hugh smiles at the inefficiency of his spreadsheet method.

> *How did I discover that the $100,000 profit target can be achieved by selling precisely 145,000 meals at our current price level? By trial and error! I completed the column for 100,000 meals and saw that the profit number was too low. Then I completed the column for 200,000 meals and saw that it was too high. So I tried various numbers between 100,000 and 200,000 until I settled on 145,000 meals.*
>
> *We're only selling 120,000 meals right now, and I don't think we can reach 145,000, so I'll need to change some assumptions. But each time I do that, I'll need to save my existing spreadsheet for future reference. What a hassle!*

Hugh jots down the following:

- Sales volume required to hit profit target is 145,000 meals
- We'll never achieve that volume; we must revisit assumptions

Hugh decides that it's time to put his spreadsheet aside and find his handy little formula. After sorting through a stack of boxes, Hugh finally locates an old book and locates it. Here it is:

Volume to Achieve Target Profit = [Target Profit + Fixed Costs in Total] / [Subtotal Per Unit]

Hugh smiles.

> *Why did I need the spreadsheet to tell me that I must sell precisely 145,000 meals to earn a $100,000 profit? My fixed costs in total are $45,000. My subtotal profit per unit is $3.50 − $2.50 = $1.00. So to earn $100,000, I need to sell [$100,000 + $45,000] / [$1.00] = 145,000 meals. Simple arithmetic.*

Hugh then calculates the volume they must sell to earn $100,000 in profits if he increases his sales price by 10%.

Well, a 35 cent increase in my price would drive up my subtotal profit per box to $1.35. So we'd need to sell [$100,000 + $45,000] / [$1.35] = 107,407 boxes. To confirm that I'm using this formula correctly, I'll complete another spreadsheet column (see Table 11.2).

Table 11.2.

	107,407 meals
Revenue @ $3.85	413,517
Variable costs @ $2.50	268,517
Subtotal	145,000
Fixed costs	45,000
Net profits	100,000

Yep, that's correct. It would have taken me a long time to settle on 107,407 with trial-and-error spreadsheet work. Thank goodness for that formula!

Now I'll relate all of these numbers back to the question at hand, which is whether we can achieve our $100,000 profit target by increasing our sales price by 10%. That would mean asking senior centers to pay a supplemental fee of 35 cents for each meal delivered to them. Heck, that's nothing . . . I'll call it a service charge and collect it easily!

Right now, at our current price level, we need to sell 145,000 meals to hit our profit target, but we're only selling 120,000 meals. If I raise my sales price by 10% by charging that 35 cent fee, our volume requirement drops from 145,000 to 107,407; that's less than the volume level we're maintaining right now!

So even if the service charge drives away a few customers, we can afford to experience a reduction in sales volume of up to 12,593 boxes (i.e., from 120,000 to 107,407) and still hit our profit target. I do believe that this plan is worth a shot.

Hugh jots down the following:

- 10% price increase drops sales volume requirement to 107,407 meals

- Can lose 12,593 meals at that price level and still hit our profit target

Looking Forward

In this chapter, we began our review of revenue estimation by using a spreadsheet approach and an arithmetic formula approach to establish price levels. This task is important to the development of the business plan because price levels are the mechanisms that establish the revenue levels required to finance all costs and generate all profits.

In the next chapter, we extend our pricing and revenue strategy to issues that extend beyond the internal cost budgets of organizations. In other words, in chapter 12, we utilize a discipline called game theory to consider whether our target prices can be maintained in the face of potential price challenges by market competitors.

CHAPTER 12

Competitive Pricing via Game Theory

About This Chapter

Chapter 12 continues our review of the revenue estimation section by explaining how the discipline of game theory can help us improve our pricing decisions by considering the decisions of our competitors. According to game theory, competitors who are using sales prices to seize customer traffic from each other are engaged in an interactive process by which external forces (i.e., the pricing decisions of others) can impact their own internal profits.

Thus, in this chapter, we explore how prices should be established under conditions of external market uncertainty. The key insight is that, under such circumstances, organizations should always analyze their situations from their competitors' perspectives before making their own pricing decisions.

Competitive Pricing via Game Theory

Your price target looks reasonable in comparison with your costs, but haven't you forgotten something? Your competitors will be watching your pricing strategy, and they'll be adjusting their own market prices to respond accordingly!

Our analysis of cost behavior helps us determine whether our pricing strategy appears to be reasonable in comparison to our cost structure, our volume capacity, and our profit requirements. But we already discussed our analysis of cost behavior in our previous chapter.

So why do we need to spend more time on our revenue plan? What else must we analyze?

The answer is simple: We must analyze the behavior of our *competitors*. After all, they are not simply going to allow us to implement our pricing strategy without a fight. They want our customers, and we want theirs; thus, we need to consider how they might set their own prices to win customer loyalty at our expense. Of course, we then need to consider how we might set our own prices to defend our business, thereby affecting our own revenue.

"Not a problem," you might say. "I'll simply guess at what my competitors will charge, and then I'll charge roughly the same price. Or perhaps I'll charge a little less, or perhaps a little more, depending on my product's reputation. Either way, it shouldn't make a big difference."

If you are thinking in these terms, though, you might be at risk of being taken to the cleaners by a competitor who knows a thing or two about game theory.

A Hand of Poker, Anyone?

Any person who plays poker—or any other competitive card game, for that matter—knows that success at the table is only partially determined by "the luck of the draw." Novices with a modicum of "beginner's luck" may nevertheless lose their shirts, whereas experienced players with mediocre hands may bluff their way into winning large stakes.

Why is this so? Such outcomes are not unusual because psychology plays a large role in the determination of success or failure. Knowledge of the opposing player plays a significant role as well. For instance, if a novice player betrays a sense of optimism and excitement whenever he holds a promising hand, his opponent will know when to walk away.

To illustrate such interactions, let's assume that you are playing a simple gambling game with a single opposing player. You and your opponent must each simultaneously raise one of your two hands. As soon as you do so, you jointly observe which hands are raised in the air—in other words, either (a) your left hand and his left hand, (b) your left hand and his right hand, (c) your right hand and his left hand, or (d) your right hand and his right hand. Then you use the chart in Table 12.1 to identify the winners and losers.

Table 12.1.

	If his left hand is raised . . .	**If his right hand is raised . . .**
If your left hand is raised . . .	You win $10; he breaks even	You win $10; he wins $10
If your right hand is raised . . .	You *lose* $20; he breaks even	You win $11; he wins $10

At first glance, most people would recommend that you should begin by raising your left hand. After all, if you do so, you are guaranteed to win $10. But if you decide to raise your right hand, you may either lose $20 or win $11. That's awfully risky; after all, you may not be able to afford a loss of $20.

In addition, considering that you have no idea how your opponent might react, you may decide to assign him a 50% chance of raising his left hand and a 50% chance of raising his right hand. That means that, if you decide to raise your right hand, your *expected value* of a 50% chance of losing $20 and a 50% chance of winning $11 is actually *negative*. Thus, raising your left hand and winning the guaranteed $10 would appear to be the preferable option.

A Self-Absorption Trap

Does this strategy sound reasonable? I hope not! If you find yourself agreeing with this stream of logic, you have regrettably fallen into a mind trap of self-absorption. To spot this trap, stop for a moment and look at the chart of winners and losers from your opponent's point of view.

That's right; take a minute and focus on his columns instead of your rows. Do you see why this strategy is wrong?

It's a fairly simple insight. If your opponent raises his left hand, he is guaranteed to break even. If he raises his right hand, he is guaranteed to win $10. So why won't he decide to raise his right hand?

Of course, that's exactly what he will always do. And once you realize that insight, you will then realize that you will always be better off raising your right hand (and *not* your left one) to lock in a $11 gain.

In a business pricing situation, of course, your opponent is your competitor, your gain is your new customer revenue, and your *left hand versus right hand* decision is actually your *full price versus discounted price* decision. The principle, though, remains the same: Whenever you analyze a situation from a competitor's point of view before choosing a course of action, you allow yourself to make an optimal choice, one that might never have occurred to you otherwise.

Applied Illustration

Hugh is participating in an experimental online auction site that matches home care service providers with private payers. Every Monday morning, providers post their visit prices on the site and then wait until noon to see what their competitors have posted. Private payers then spend the remainder of the day purchasing services for the remainder of the week.

Hugh has recently lost sales volume to very small independent home care workers who can afford to undercut his agency's prices; he is considering a plan to heavily discount his own prices, at least temporarily, in order to win back payer loyalty. Hugh realizes, though, that the "independents" are a close-knit group of entrepreneurs who jointly promote their home-grown business enterprises. He suspects that they are considering further discounting activities.

Hugh considers the impact on sales if he and his competitors (a) hold prices firm for their services or (b) offer heavily discounted prices. He says,

Unfortunately, I doubt that we have any real chance of attracting any consumers back from the independents. We lost them long ago because they always wanted friendly, informal service, something we simply can't provide as a heavily regulated organization.

Nevertheless, we can certainly lose additional consumers to the independents if we make mistakes with our pricing; although most of our consumers prefer to receive care from professional service organizations like ours, they might nevertheless be attracted to slightly cheaper alternatives. Alternatively, under certain circumstances, we might pick up some business if we can convince people who aren't yet purchasing any home care services at all to give us a try.

So let me draft up a table to analyze our options. I'm pretty sure that we'll attract 30 consumers who aren't receiving any services at all if we discount our prices. In fact, as long as those pesky independents don't slash their prices, we'll probably attract them anyway because we're investing in various direct marketing activities. But if the independents catch us by surprise and further underprice our services, we'll probably lose 10 consumers to them if we don't respond accordingly. We'll probably also lose another 10 consumers who will think of us as "price hogs" and will simply decide to go without home care services for a while.

Based on this information, Hugh develops Table 12.2.
Hugh says,

Well, our choice seems pretty clear. We should simply guarantee ourselves an increase of 30 consumers by offering discounts. But before we do that, let me ask myself whether our decision may change if we assess the situation from the point of view of the independents.

Hugh jots down the following:

- Can we assure ourselves volume increases by discounting prices?
- But what about the competitor's perspective?

The independents provide a highly popular, informal service option with a book of business that is expanding by 10 consumers per month; as long as they adhere to their business model, I don't believe we can change their growth trend. But if they begin to offer deeper discounts, all bets are off. They might actually lose consumers if their core market becomes convinced that they are trying to attract large

Table 12.2.

	Independents offer discount	Independents hold prices firm
Hugh offers discount	Hugh +30.	Hugh +30.
Hugh holds prices firm	Hugh −20.	Hugh +30.

amounts of consumers from us and are thus becoming large and bureaucratic places themselves.

So, if the independents discount their prices, I think they might find themselves sustaining no natural growth at all. Sure, they might pick up our 10 consumers if we hold our prices firm, but I don't think they'd pry any additional consumers from us if we match their discounts.

And thus Hugh prepares the schedule seen in Table 12.3.
Hugh says,

Wow! I'm glad that I thought about this from their point of view before deciding to discount our prices. I now see that the independents have no reason to discount their prices; as long as they maintain a full price policy, we should do so as well.

Sure, we'd still pick up 30 new consumers if we slash our prices while the independents hold prices firm. But if we do that, the independents might feel threatened by us, and our consumers might start expecting deeper discounts in the future. Unless we can actually generate more volume-based revenue by slashing our prices, we're better off maintaining a full price psychology throughout our industry segment.

Hugh jots down the following:

- Only possibility of loss when we hold prices firm and they offer discounts
- A benefit to maintaining full price psychology

Table 12.3.

	Independents offer discount	Independents hold prices firm
Hugh offers discount	Hugh +30; independents +0.	Hugh +30; independents +10.
Hugh holds prices firm	Hugh −20; independents +10.	Hugh +30; independents +10.

Looking Forward

In this chapter, we continued our review of revenue estimation by employing game theory to reassess pricing strategies after considering the pricing activities of our competitors. This task is important to the development of the business plan because price levels are not solely dictated by internal cost and target profit considerations; in fact, heavy discounting may be required whenever competitors threaten to seize our customers and reduce our volumes.

In the next chapter, we conclude our discussion of pricing and revenue strategy by considering situations where price wars are relatively likely. In other words, in chapter 13, we address situations where prices must be slashed as low as possible, and discounts offered to as many consumers as possible, in order to preserve sales volume and market share.

CHAPTER 13

Price-Discounting Strategies

About This Chapter

Chapter 13 concludes our review of the revenue estimation section by explaining how organizations should establish the scope, and the limits, of their price-discounting strategies. Although most organizations prefer to avoid situations where discounting is necessary, entrepreneurs must be prepared to consider such strategies if aggressive competition makes it necessary to implement them.

Thus, in this chapter, we explore how prices should be established under conditions of severe external market threats. As we originally established with our discussion of variable and fixed costs in chapter 11, considerations of cost behavior greatly impact how deeply prices can be slashed under such circumstances.

Price-Discounting Strategies

Do you know what I valued most about your cost analysis? It was your variance work; it convinced me that you've thought about how you'd handle vendor cost spikes and other unexpected events. But what about unexpected events that affect your revenues? Have you thought about them as well?

Sooner or later, it happens to every well-managed business. A desperate competitor stumbles to the brink of bankruptcy and decides to slash prices to liquidate inventory. Or a new rival entering the market decides to give away their services at absurdly low introductory prices. When price wars beckon, how should organizations respond?

It is, of course, extremely difficult to plan appropriate responses in advance. Sometimes it is better to simply maintain one's prices and hope that the new threat dissipates in the near future. But other times, the deep discounter gains traction and begins to siphon business away from firms that are well established in the industry. Even worse, sometimes customers begin to expect deep discounts from industry players and thus become unwilling to pay full prices under any conditions.

It is thus impossible to craft a comprehensive response plan that can address all contingencies. Nevertheless, it is certainly possible (and, in fact, beneficial) to establish a general policy regarding special discounting strategies. No revenue section of a business plan can be considered complete without some evaluation of the circumstances that might trigger temporary price reductions as well as some discussion regarding the extent to which prices might be slashed accordingly.

Assessing Customer Loyalty

When a price war appears on the horizon, we must critically assess the levels of loyalty that existing customers (as well as potential target customers) maintain toward our organization. Ironically, the more loyal our customer base, the less pressure we'll feel to surrender revenue by offering price discounts to maintain our market share.

Let's assume, for instance, that we believe we have a fairly strong business relationship with our current customer base. However, let's assume that we've been pursuing a target group of new customers, and we're concerned that we might fail to establish a strong market presence in their sector because of a competitor's lower prices. Under such circumstances, we may be willing to institute a *special introductory price* discount for new customers, a price that barely covers the out-of-pocket costs of serving our new customers. Such a strategy may be attractive because it would allow us to continue maintaining our existing profit levels on our current base of customers.

However, if we are concerned about the possibility of losing some of our current customers to a low-priced competitor, we might need to become far more aggressive in slashing our own prices. Under such circumstances, we may decide to *slash prices across the board* for all customers, even if we must sacrifice all of our profits in the short term. No for-profit business could afford to sacrifice all of its profits in the long term, but as an immediate competitive pricing strategy, it might be necessary (and, in fact, desirable) to do so.

Using Cost Behavior

The cost behavior data in the revenue section of the business plan provides the information that is required to establish the appropriate price level for each of these strategies. In order to recoup the out-of-pocket costs of serving *new* customers, it would be necessary to charge them (i.e., the new customers only) a price that is equal to the *variable costs per unit* of doing business with them. And in order to sacrifice all profits and yet maintain a break-even zero profit position on *all* customers, it would be necessary to charge them (i.e., all of the customers, the new as well as the old) a price that is equal to the sum of the *variable costs per unit and the fixed costs per unit.*

Is it ever desirable to establish discounted price levels that are even lower than these options, in other words, to intentionally sell products and services at a loss? It may be necessary to do so under very limited circumstances and for very short periods of time, but only when absolutely necessary. There may be alternative options that are available to businesses that find themselves in such circumstances, such as filing regulatory complaints against foreign firms that may be pricing their goods illegally in local markets, or asking state governments to institute sales tax holidays that lower the effective prices paid by customers without reducing revenues collected by the firms.

Applied Illustration

Hugh manages a postnatal home care service under contract with a local hospital. The hospital pays Hugh's agency to provide home-based health services to postpartum mothers and their newborn infants on an "as needed" basis for 1 month after their discharge dates; then Hugh offers an optional 11 month continuation service that is paid directly by the families.

Hugh has always assumed that his contractual affiliation with the hospital would protect him from any competition, but he has recently learned that a rival home care agency has begun selling a home-based service as well. The hospital's contract only extends coverage for the limited 1-month period; Hugh's agency then offers consumers an additional 11 months of coverage for a flat fee. The rival agency, though, has begun informing consumers that they can reduce their costs by using Hugh's service for the first month and then purchasing deeply discounted services from the rival agency for the following 11 months.

Hugh realizes that he may need to institute a discounted price arrangement in order to maintain his current consumers throughout the 12-month period. Although all discharged mothers and babies automatically receive 1 month of service coverage, most go on to purchase extended coverage as well, and many become consumers of numerous other programs and services. Thus, Hugh's entire revenue structure would be vulnerable if the rival agency succeeds.

Hugh is currently maintaining a book of business with 1,000 consumers. He recently prepared a cost behavior spreadsheet for insertion in his business plan, one that included $500 as an average price for the 11 months of service coverage, $100 as the average variable cost per consumer of providing the service, and $300,000 as the fixed cost of maintaining the administrative infrastructure of the program (see Table 13.1).

Hugh reviews his spreadsheet and thinks,

Hmm. The majority of our cost structure appears to be fixed in nature. That makes sense because many mothers and babies are relatively healthy and need very few visits. Thus, our administrative activities tend to dominate our income statement.

That being the situation, I think we can afford to become very aggressive in launching a special teaser price for new consumers as long as we manage to maintain our current profit levels from our existing consumers. I doubt that any of our existing consumers will try to break their contracts with us.

Table 13.1.

	900 consumers	1,000 consumers	1,100 consumers
Revenue @ $500	450,000	500,000	550,000
Variable costs @ $100	90,000	100,000	110,000
Subtotal	360,000	400,000	440,000
Fixed costs	300,000	300,000	300,000
Net profits	60,000	100,000	140,000

Hugh jots down the following:

- High fixed costs, low variable costs
- Current base of customers is stable

Right now, we are serving 1,000 consumers and earning a profit of $100,000. Let's say that we decide to establish an aggressive discounted teaser price for new customers that is equal to our variable cost per unit of $100. That is a discount of 80% off our current standard price; it should send our new competitor a signal that we mean business. If we then pick up 100 new consumers and charge them a price of $100, we should still be able to maintain our current overall profit level of $100,000 (see Table 13.2).

Hugh checked his numbers (see Table 13.2).

Hugh jots down the following:

- Can maintain profit levels with 80% teaser price discount
- Assuming teaser price is offered to new customers only

I think that'll be an effective strategy, but what if it doesn't drive our rival away from our business? Or what if our current consumers start to break their contracts and defect to our rival for the remaining portion of their 11-month term? I suppose we should then consider establishing an everyday low price policy and extend it to all of our customers. If we have 1,100 customers at that time, our new price would need to be the variable cost per unit of $100 plus the fixed cost per unit of $273 (i.e., $300,000 divided by 1,100); in other words, we'd charge everyone $373.

Table 13.2.

	First 1,000 consumers	Next 100 consumers	Total
Revenue @ $500/$100	500,000	10,000	510,000
Variable costs @ $100	100,000	10,000	110,000
Subtotal	400,000	0	400,000
Fixed costs	300,000	0	300,000
Net profits	100,000	0	100,000

Hugh checked his numbers as follows (see Table 13.3)

Table 13.3

	1,100 consumers
Revenue @ $373	410,000
Variable costs @ $100	110,000
Subtotal	300,000
Fixed costs	300,000
Net profits	0

Hugh reviews these numbers and exclaims,

Ouch! A profit of zero is going to hurt. Nevertheless, at least I now know how low we can go without dropping into the red if we decide to establish an everyday low price policy for all of our consumers.

You know, I recently heard that our rival is thinking about undercutting our $500 price with a 20% discount to $400. Well, perhaps we should go ahead and blow them out of the water with a $100 teaser price for new consumers. If that doesn't scare our rival away, we'll undercut their $400 price with a $373 price for everyone. Current consumers should enjoy seeing their prices slashed from $500 to $373, and new consumers who complete their initial 1 month period should enjoy the news that their rate will only increase to $373 and not to $500 (or even $400). They may decide to drop their service entirely, but at least they won't go to our competitor for $400 when they can stay with us for $373.

Hugh jots down the following:

- Can afford to go as low as $373 as an *everyday low price* policy
- Assuming we grow our book of business to 1,100 consumers

Looking Forward

In this chapter, we concluded our review of revenue estimation by returning to our analysis of cost behavior to determine price-discounting strategies in the face of severe market competition. This task is important to the development of the business plan because an immediate and highly aggressive price-discounting strategy can often serve as an effective weapon for preventing rivals from gaining a foothold in our market.

In the next chapter, we begin our discussion of investment value by using our volume, cost, and revenue estimates to construct a full set of financial accounting statements. In other words, in chapter 14, we use the information that we developed in the previous parts of our business plan to develop a comprehensive fiscal snapshot of the health of our organization.

PART VI

Investment Value

CHAPTER 14

Cash Flow Analysis

About This Chapter

Chapter 14 begins our review of the investment value section by describing the three financial statements and then focusing on the statement of cash flows. All three statements are important because it is possible to be immensely profitable and yet go bankrupt; entrepreneurs must plan carefully to avoid such catastrophes.

Thus, in this chapter, we explore how financial statements should be constructed to assess the equity value of an organization as well as the extent in which it is earning profits and cash flows. We also address differences between operating, investing, and financing cash flows and describe how to calculate them by utilizing balance sheet and income statement data.

Cash Flow Analysis

Well, you certainly appear to be developing a profitable business concept. But have you thought about your cash flow needs? Even the most profitable companies can get caught without cash on the day they distribute paychecks or make debt payments. Is that going to be a problem for you?

We've all seen them from time to time: People who drive luxury automobiles and then bounce checks, billionaires who borrow small change to buy breath mints, and commuter train riders who admit to conductors, "I don't have the cash to buy my ticket."

It happens to the wealthiest of individuals. But when it happens to a firm, terrible consequences may follow. A failure to make a debt payment may result in the seizure of assets pledged as collateral, the same assets that may be required to maintain operations. And a failure to meet payroll may result in the outright closure of operations.

Thus, whenever organizations develop their profit estimates, they must also plan their cash flow projections. Both sets of targets—in other words, both accrual and cash *income* goals—must be monitored closely to ensure the fiscal health of the firm.

Three Statements for Three Needs

All organizations have three specific financial planning needs that must be met on a continuing basis. First, they need to know that the value of their resources will exceed the value of their obligations at any given *moment* in time. Second, they need to know that they will achieve their accrual income goals over any given *period* of time. And third, they need to know that they will not run shy of cash during that same *period* of time.

Fortunately for business planners, our colleagues in accounting have designed a statement to serve each need. The *balance sheet*, for instance, tallies up assets and compares them to liabilities to ensure that the organization's equity value is positive. The *income statement* tallies up revenues and then subtracts expenses to calculate net income or profits. And the *cash flow statement* tallies up three different types of cash flows—financing, investing, and operating cash flows, to be precise—that produce the cash asset balance that appears on the balance sheet.

Financing cash flows encompass any receipts or disbursements that are related to raising or repaying capital; they include cash received from loan borrowings and stock issuances, as well as cash payments on loan balances and dividend agreements. Investing cash flows encompass any fixed asset purchases that are required to prepare for future growth.

Neither of these cash flows, though, encompasses the thousands of small cash transactions that organizations make daily to operate their businesses. Purchasing and selling inventory, paying vendors and workers, receiving cash from customers . . . these are all classified as operating cash flows.

How much of each type of cash flow is required to run a successful business? There is no single answer to this question; the amounts vary from industry to industry and from organization to organization. A start-up software business that is developing applications for corporate clients might produce negative operating cash flows for several years while relying on positive financing cash flows from private investors. On the other hand, a small residential home builder with no external sources of capital might eliminate all investing cash flow activities when its operating cash flows turn negative.

Applied Illustration

Hugh's home care agency offers home-based dialysis services to consumers with kidney disease. As a concurrent service, he also stocks and sells home dialysis machines at a reasonable profit; he is now considering several options for expansion of the machine-distribution business.

One option is to spend $20,000 on renovations to expand the machine warehouse for future growth; however, Hugh's banker is pressuring him to first repay 75% of the loan that he incurred when he opened for business. Taken together, these two requirements would require him to spend $50,000, which is quite a sum for the machine distribution division. But Hugh isn't worried; the division began the year with $50,000 in cash and has been profitable since then.

Still, Hugh intends to prepare a set of financial statements to assess whether the division's assets will exceed its liabilities at the end of the year and to project whether its accrual and cash incomes will remain positive over the course of the year. So he begins by reviewing the division's balance sheet from the first day of the year (in thousands of dollars) (see Table 14.1).

Then Hugh jots down some expectations about the year. He expects to average $10,000 (retail value) of machine sales monthly and $7,000 (cost value) of machine purchases monthly. He also expects to spend $1,000 monthly on marketing activities.

Table 14.1.

Cash	50	Payables	20
Receivables	20	Bank debt	40
Inventory	10		
Building	20	Equity	40
Total	100	Total	100

His customers all buy on credit and take 3 months to pay their invoices; thus, he does not expect any write-offs of receivables. His machine inventory sits in the warehouse for 2 months until they are purchased by customers; thus, he does not expect any write-offs of inventory either.

Hugh plans to pay 50% of his vendor payables by year-end as well as 75% of his bank loan. To maintain the value of his depreciating (at a rate of $5,000 annually) warehouse, he plans to spend $20,000 at year-end on renovations. In addition, Hugh's lender has agreed to a simple interest arrangement; an annual interest fee of 10% is charged on any balance that is outstanding at year-end.

So, with this information in hand, Hugh prepares the year-end balance sheet projections (in thousands of dollars; see Table 14.2).

Then he prepares the income statement projections (in thousands of dollars; Table 14.3).

Hugh thinks, *Good! We're still highly profitable. We expect to earn $18,000 on sales of $120,000; that's a positive net margin of 15%. So our balance sheet equity value should soar from $40,000 to $58,000 by year-end . . . that's a spectacular 45% gain!*

Table 14.2.

Cash	*	Payables (50% of 20)	10
Receivables (3 months @ $10)	30	Bank debt (25% of 40)	10
Inventory (2 months @ $7)	14		
Building (20 – 5 + 20)	35	Equity	*
Total	*	Total	*

* Note: to be determined

Table 14.3.

Sales (12 months @ $10)	120
Cost of sales (12 months @ $7)	84
Gross profit	36
Marketing (12 months @ $1)	12
Depreciation (on original building)	5
Interest (10% of $10)	1
Net income	18

Hugh jots down the following:

- Accrual income profits
- 15% net margin, 45% equity increases

Then Hugh prepares his cash flow spreadsheet (in thousands of dollars; see Table 14.4).

Now Hugh says,

Hmm. Those negative numbers in the "$ impact" column are a bit worrisome. But I'm sure they're correct; I didn't make any mistakes. When assets increase, it's generally bad for cash because we need to spend cash to buy or finance them. And when liabilities decrease, it's also bad for cash because we need to spend cash to pay them down.

Now I'll sort those "$ impact" numbers into the three cash flow categories. We began the year with $50,000 in cash, so I'm not worried . . . I think we can afford to burn through a bit of it.

Hugh then prepares his cash flow statement projections . . . and he is stunned to see his bottom line (in thousands of dollars; see Table 14.5).

Hugh exclaims, *My goodness! Am I projecting a $1,000 overdrawn cash balance by year-end? That can't be possible! Let's plug that negative $1,000 cash number into the year-end balance sheet projection and see if it balances.*

Table 14.4.

	Begins @	Ends @	Change	$ impact
Receivables	20	30	10	–10
Inventory	10	14	4	–4
Building (original)	20	15	–5	5
Building (renovations)	0	20	20	–20
Payables	20	10	–10	–10
Bank debt	40	10	–30	–30
Equity	40	58	18	18

Table 14.5.

Equity (net income)	18
Building (depreciation)	5
Receivables	−10
Inventory	−4
Payables	−10
Subtotal (operating cash flows)	−1
Building renovations (investing cash flows)	−20
Bank debt (financing cash flows)	−30
Change in cash during year	−51
Cash at beginning of year	50
Cash at end of year	−1

So Hugh prepares his year-end balance sheet projection and is dumb-founded by the results (in thousands of dollars; see Table 14.6).

Hugh sighs. *Yes, it's correct. If we continue down this path, this division is bankrupt by the end of the year.*

Hugh jots down the following:

- Bankruptcy
- Negative $1,000 operating cash flow; negative $50,000 other cash flows

I guess I should be relieved that I decided to develop this plan. Let me think about this situation. On an operational basis, we're allowing receivables and inventory to creep up by $10,000 and $4,000, respectively. When our consumers take longer to pay their bills, and when

Table 14.6.

Cash	−1	Payables	10
Receivables	30	Bank Debt	10
Inventory	14		
Building	35	Equity	58
Total	78	Total	78

inventory piles up on shelves, our cash flows suffer the consequences, so these factors are bad for cash.

We're also planning to pay down our vendor balances by $10,000; though our vendors may appreciate our payments, this is also bad for cash. So even though we're earning cash income of $23,000, we're also frittering away $24,000, and thus we're stuck with a net operating cash flow loss of $1,000.

Is that a big deal? At first I thought not, considering that we began the year with $50,000 in the bank. But we won't end the year with $49,000 in the bank because we're planning to spend $20,000 on renovations and $30,000 on loan repayments. That seemed reasonable when we assumed that our operating cash flows were positive, but now I see that it makes no sense whatsoever.

Hugh breathes deeply and thinks about his next steps:

I'll need to tell our lender that a 75% repayment transaction is out of the question. At the very least, we'll need to cut back on our renovations budget as well. And we should rethink our cost and revenue structures to eke out some additional accrual and cash income from our operational activities.

Hugh certainly has his work cut out for him. But because of his initiative to estimate his future cash flows, he won't be caught by surprise.

Hugh jots down the following:

- Eliminate debt repayments; reduce renovations
- Rethink costs, revenues

Looking Forward

In this chapter, we began our review of revenue estimation by reviewing a case illustration involving a firm that is highly profitable and yet is heading for bankruptcy; we are able to detect and address such problems through the creation of financial statements. This task is important to the development of the business plan because the investment value of highly profitable organizations may be impaired if the organizations encounter significant cash flow problems.

In the next chapter, we continue our discussion of investment value by discussing performance measurements that are calculated with data that appear on these financial statements. In other words, in chapter 15, we use the information that appears on the three financial statements to calculate statistics such as return on equity (ROE) and residual income (RI).

CHAPTER 15

Financial Ratio Analysis

About This Chapter

Chapter 15 continues our review of the investment value section by exploring the topic of ratio analysis. The purpose of ratio analysis is to measure the value of an organization, and by extension the value of investments that have been made in an organization, through the use of statistics that are calculated with information that can be found within the financial statements.

Thus, in this chapter, we explore the calculation of a pair of financial ratios and discuss their application to issues of business planning and management. Although there are thousands of financial ratios that are commonly utilized throughout the global economy, we focus on two well-established statistics: return on equity (ROE) and residual income (RI).

Financial Ratio Analysis

I appreciate your hard work in creating the financial statements. Many people, though, don't have the time, the need, the knowledge, or the experience to pore through them and absorb all the details. Can you create a few summary ratios to help your own managers understand their goals?

Sophisticated parties will scrutinize a firm's financial statement projections to assess whether its plan is practical and feasible. Its operations managers, though, may not need to become avid readers of that set of data. Nevertheless, they do require clear operational targets that are expressed in simple business language, targets that reflect the underlying fiscal goals of the enterprise.

There are various methods for converting voluminous financial statement information into concise business targets. Two of the most commonly known techniques are known as return on equity (ROE) and residual income (RI).

Return on Equity (ROE)

In our previous chapter, we noted that three distinct financial statements serve to answer three specific questions about an organization. ROE possesses a similar structure; it is composed of three distinct statistical indicators that serve to provide business targets for three specific operational functions.

What are these functions? Let's think about a traditional manufacturing company. To achieve its goals, it must hire property development specialists to purchase land and construct factories. Then it must hire salesmen to sell products to customers. Finally, it must hire plant managers to produce those products in their factories.

That's a very basic strategy, isn't it? In fact, the people who manage each of these functions can simply focus on their own tasks and leave the other activities to their colleagues. In modern corporations, these managers don't need to know each other at all in order to tend to their own responsibilities. They don't need to work in the same offices or mingle at company meetings either. As long as the property development team is visiting prospective factory sites, the sales team is backslapping customers, and the plant management team is supervising factory operations, the firm should be able to achieve prosperity through the segregation of duties and the specialization of business functions.

The performance of each function within this triumvirate can be judged accordingly on the basis of its own financial performance statistic. Over the past century, many different versions of such statistics have been developed; one popular example is the three-part ROE indicator, which can be described in the following manner.

The property development team's goal is to maximize the amount of factory assets developed in comparison to the size of the firm; thus, its goal is to maximize the value of the fraction assets /equity.

In other words . . . as the firm grows, its equity value grows, too . . . and expectations about the amount of factory assets that must be developed will grow as well.

The sales team's goal is to maximize the amount of products that are sold to customers after being manufactured within the factory assets; thus, its goal is to maximize the value of the fraction sales/assets.

In other words . . . as the firm's base of factory assets grows, its production capacity grows, too . . . and expectations about the amount of sales needed to distribute those products will grow as well.

The plant management team's goal is to minimize the costs that are incurred, and thus maximize the profits that are earned, by producing the products that are sold to customers; thus, its goal is to maximize the value of the fraction profits/sales.

In other words . . . as the firm's book of business grows, it must keep its production costs low even as its sales increase . . . and thus profits will grow accordingly.

What happens if we multiply these three fractions together? Well, the assets and sales numbers cancel out of the numerators and denominators, leaving us with the fraction profits/equity.

Does that fraction look familiar? You might recognize it as the investment community's favorite statistic, ROE.

In fact, this is the primary value of the ROE calculation. As you can see, when each of the three functions maximize the value of its own statistical target, the resulting increases in each of their fractions will lead to (when multiplied together) the maximization of ROE as well.

Residual Income (RI)

ROE is a helpful technique, but it doesn't explain in precise terms how organizations should reward or punish their managers for achieving (or failing to achieve) their financial objectives. At what point should managers expect to receive bonuses for superior performance? Or warnings for inferior performance? It is obviously beneficial to tie such incentives directly to statistical targets.

RI is a technique that is designed to answer these questions. Simply put, a manager whose divisional performance falls below his firm's minimum RI expectations may expect to receive a warning, be placed on probation, or be dismissed. At the other end of the spectrum, a manager who exceeds his firm's maximum RI expectations may expect to receive praise, be given additional responsibilities, or be promoted to a higher position.

A firm's minimum RI expectation (i.e., MIN-RI) is equal to the difference between the actual profits that a division earns and the *minimum* profits that the firm expects it to earn on the basis of its original investment. When actual profits exceed minimum expectations, then MIN-RI is positive and no warning is delivered to the manager. But when actual profits fall short of minimum expectations, then MIN-RI is negative and the manager is warned accordingly.

A firm's maximum RI expectation (i.e., MAX-RI), on the other hand, is equal to the difference between the actual profits that a division earns and the *superior (or at least average)* profits that the firm expects it to earn during a specific period of time. When actual profits exceed superior (or at least average) expectations, then MAX-RI is positive and the manager is rewarded accordingly. But when actual profits fall short of superior (or at least average) expectations, then MAX-RI is negative and no reward is delivered to the manager.

As long as MIN-RI is negative, then MAX-RI must be negative as well. And as long as MAX-RI is positive, then MIN-RI must be positive as well. Furthermore, organizations that grade their managers in a *bell curve* fashion (so that most managers fall in the middle of the performance spectrum) establish their minimum and average expectations so that MIN-RI is positive and MAX-RI is negative for most managers.

Applied Illustration

Hugh's home care agency has just closed its books for the year; now it is time to compute annual performance statistics. There are three senior vice presidents who report to Hugh: (a) a Chief Information Officer (CIO) who oversees the clinical and financial hardware, software, and telecommunications infrastructure, (b) a Chief Business Development Officer (CBDO) who manages all sales activities, and (c) a Chief Operations Officer (COO) who manages all nursing service activities. As a management accountant by training, Hugh serves as his own Chief Financial Officer.

The agency's closing balance sheet contains $10 million in assets, most of which are information systems and telecommunications hardware, as well as $6 million in liabilities and $4 million in equity. Its income statement for the year contains $5 million in sales revenue and $4 million in operating expenses, yielding $1 million in profits.

Hugh begins his year-end assessment work by calculating his ROE fractions. The CIO's division produced a performance statistic of 2.5

Times Equity (i.e., \$10 / \$4), the CBDO's division produced a statistic of 50% (i.e., \$5 / \$10), and the COO's division produced a statistic of 20% (i.e., [\$5 – \$4] / \$5). Thus, ROE equaled 25% (i.e., \$1 / \$4, or 2.5 times 50% times 20%). These percentages all appeared in line with historical norms, so Hugh simply noted the information in his annual report.

Hugh jots down the following:

- ROE averaging a healthy 25%
- Each division appears strong as well

Then Hugh proceeds to focus on a more specific task, one involving a line of luxury services that was recently developed for affluent private pay consumers. Hugh's agency generally focuses on the mass market, but he decided to try establishing a hybrid health spa and home care service unit in a Class A office building early last year. Hugh also created a special sales team to work closely with the operations team to customize their services to meet refined tastes. The agency invested heavily in this initiative, hoping for a significant return on their investment.

Hugh gathers his data together and says:

Let's analyze that line's performance. It earned \$100,000 in profits; hey, at first glance, that's pretty impressive! But we originally invested \$1 million to develop the line, and our minimum Return on Investment (ROI) for any new project is 8%.

Hugh gathered other information as well. At year-end, the health spa contained \$2 million of undepreciated assets and \$900,000 in related mortgage liabilities. Furthermore, the firm's average cost of capital during the year was 12%.

Hugh says,

Okay, let's find out if the genius who proposed this new line is going to get promoted or fired. MIN-RI is the difference between \$100,000 and 8% of \$1 million; that's positive \$20,000. Well, I guess he'll keep his job!

Now let's move on to MAX-RI. Although we originally invested $1 million in the line, we generally use net assets as the basis of our MAX-RI calculation, which is equal to $1.1 million (i.e., $2 million minus $900,000). So MAX-RI is the difference between $100,000 and 12% of $1.1 million; that's negative $32,000. Hmm; I guess there's no bonus for him!

But wait; I've noticed something interesting. If we had used the original investment number of $1 million in our MAX-RI calculation instead of the net asset number of $1.1 million, MAX-RI would still be negative, but it would be a lot closer to zero; it would be negative $20,000, to be precise. Perhaps we should consider creating different versions of MAX-RI (as well as MIN-RI, for that matter) for different purposes in the future.

Hugh jots down the following:

- Positive MIN-RI and Negative MAX-RI
- No warning, but no bonus either
- Consider alternative calculations

Looking Forward

In this chapter, we continued our review of investment value by reviewing a pair of financial ratios that are designed to assess the overall fiscal health of an organization, as well as the health of the divisions that operate within it. This task is important to the development of the business plan because firmwide investment values can fluctuate significantly from period to period, and are often greatly impacted by conditions that occur within just one or two areas of the organization.

In the next chapter, we conclude our discussion of investment value by discussing performance measurements that are nonfinancial in nature. In other words, in chapter 16, we extend our collection of performance measurements to include qualitative (as well as nonfinancial quantitative) data that assess the value of an organization.

CHAPTER 16

Outcomes Management and Measurement

About This Chapter

Chapter 16 concludes our review of the investment value section by further exploring the field of outcomes management and measurement. The financial ratios that were discussed in chapter 15 are actually valid examples of this topic; in this chapter, however, we extend our discussion to qualitative and nonfiscal quantitative measurements as well.

Thus, in this chapter, we discuss how entrepreneurs can produce such data and incorporate them into dashboard reports for management purposes. We also describe a pair of methodologies for developing such reports: one emphasizing the process chain of the organization and another emphasizing the business plan of the entity.

Outcomes Management and Measurement

Your financial statements and ratios will certainly help you monitor your fiscal status. In fact, I'm quite comfortable with the quantitative goals in your plan, but what about the qualitative goals? Are you planning to keep track of any nonfinancial indicators of success as well?

Congratulations! You're reaching the end of the business-planning process, but you have a few more issues to address before you can finalize your work. You've already analyzed your revenue, cost, and investment estimates, as well as the business model and volume expectations that support them. You've also completed your financial statement projections and have added a set of financial targets. But you haven't yet described your nonfinancial targets.

Qualitative outcome measurements are an important part of any business plan because they serve as canaries in a coal mine, identifying barriers to success that may mushroom into crises if they are not addressed promptly and effectively. Are your customers holding longer than usual while on the telephone to reach your customer service representatives? They may decide to be patient for a little while, but negative word of mouth will eventually damage your financial health by inflicting losses of sales revenue. Or are you rejecting abnormally large batches of vendor raw materials because of spoilage while in transit? The cost might be negligible in the short term, but it might accumulate to a significant amount in the long term, especially if the problem worsens over time.

How should these qualitative performance indicators be reported to senior officers? Many organizations create a *dashboard report*, with icons and graphic images arranged on a screen or page in much the same manner that warning lights are arranged on an automobile dashboard. Colors such as red, yellow, and green can be used to differentiate between major concerns, minor concerns, and nonconcerns; furthermore, arrows can be used to portray directional trends, such as improving or worsening conditions.

These details are simply a matter of appearance, of course; what matters more is the content of the underlying data that is collected and reviewed for control purposes. But how do firms select data items for collection? And how do they decide when fluctuations in those items should trigger a red or yellow light on a dashboard report?

Process Chain Methodology

One approach to selecting items for qualitative tracking involves the use of the process chain methodology that was described in the first section of the business plan. In a sense, this approach requires us to come full circle and achieve a degree of closure by reconfirming the central tenets that underlie our entire plan.

As you may recall, the process chain methodology requires us to define our organizational strategy in terms of four factors: people, work activities, customers, and sources of capital. It challenges us to express our strategy by describing how key employees focus on critical work activities, thereby satisfying specific groups of target customers and earning sufficient profits to repay our sources of capital. The best business plans are successful because they begin with very specific descriptions of these four factors, and they explain the interdependencies between them.

Many organizations select one or more qualitative measurements that address each of these factors and continually review their outcome data to ensure that the process chain remains relevant and strong. A municipality's mass transportation system, for instance, might define its process chain as one that focuses on (a) engineers keeping equipment breakdowns to a minimum through (b) the use of preventive maintenance techniques so that (c) customers can arrive at their destinations safely while (d) paying minimal fares.

If this is the chain, then the system might define their indicators of success as (a) the effectiveness of engineer training activities, (b) the number of equipment breakdowns, (c) the extent to which customers express satisfaction with the reliability of the service, and (d) the amount of time that passes between fare hikes. Some of these indicators are qualitative in nature and some are quantitative in nature; together, they represent a comprehensive set of nonfinancial targets of success.

Business Plan Methodology

An alternative approach is to utilize the sections of the business plan itself to define the qualitative data that is collected by our organization. Although this method does not quite permit us to come full circle in the same sense that we do when utilizing the process chain methodology, we nevertheless must review all of the sections of our plan in order to implement this approach.

In a sense, our business plan methodology literally encompasses a process chain methodology because the process chain itself is described in a major section of the plan. However, when utilizing a business plan methodology, the process chain and other elements of the business model only provide a single cluster of one or more qualitative measurements. The volume, cost, revenue, and investment value sections also provide equally important and relevant clusters of measurements.

By using such an approach, a municipal mass transportation system might decide that (a) its greatest volume challenge is minimizing the time that passengers must wait for trains on platforms, (b) its greatest cost challenge is minimizing its overtime pay to train drivers and conductors, (c) its greatest revenue challenge is convincing passengers to purchase monthly passes instead of single fare tokens, and (d) its greatest investment valuation challenge is negotiating payment terms with vendors that permit delays of 60 to 90 days before payments are due. Under such circumstances, the nonfinancial measurements to be tracked might include (a) platform waiting times, (b) overtime hours worked, (c) passenger survey results, and (d) days in accounts payable.

Applied Illustration

One of the most challenging business contracts that Hugh has signed during the past several years is a nurse staffing arrangement with a drugstore that maintains a primary care walk-in clinic behind its cash register area. The building was originally built in the early 20th century to accommodate a small manufacturer; although the facilities have been renovated on numerous occasions to accommodate patient flow, the cramped nature of the building has always been the subject of numerous complaints about the poor quality of the patient experience.

Hugh decides to design and implement a dashboard report that will help him identify various concerns that can be addressed by his operations management team. He begins his work by reviewing his process chain analysis.

Hugh muses,

Let's see what we developed when we first initiated our planning process. Hmm. It appears that we identified the receptionist lines as the cause of the worst patient experiences in our clinic. Well, that makes perfect sense because our facility was originally designed and built as a small manufacturing facility well before any one foresaw the need for waiting rooms and medical record areas. We've tried our best to cram everything into the available space, but when those receptionist lines back up, the arriving walk-in patients have no place to go.

Receptionist line delays also affect the process flow analysis that we included in the volume section of our business plan. When there are delays at the reception desk, passengers tend to bottleneck in the waiting room seating area. Then we try our best to alleviate those bottlenecks by adding one or two student workers to the reception desk, but the treatment rooms still experience terrible crowding effects when the bottlenecked patients are finally checked in and are then rushed in and out of the clinical treatment stations.

Because of traffic problems and other external uncertainties, we never really know in advance how many reception personnel are needed to staff the desk during any given period. That plays havoc with the variance analyses in the cost section of our plan because we need to keep extra student workers available to work on short notice for additional pay. And our revenues are impacted as well because some health insurers pay us higher fees for long visits than for short visits. We lose revenue when passengers are kept waiting in line and are thus squeezed in during short visit sessions when their symptoms and conditions might justify longer visits.

Well, after considering these matters, I've decided that we should focus all of our outcome measurements on the receptionist lines, at least for the time being. I'll have to explain that my decision shouldn't be interpreted as a sign of indifference about problems elsewhere; rather, it simply reflects my belief that the underlying cause of many other problems can be traced back to the receptionist lines.

Hugh jots down the following:

- Focus on receptionist line bottlenecks
- Causes problems throughout the facility

I believe that the process chain and the business plan methodologies each have merit, so I'd like to use both of them to select my qualitative criteria. First, let me think about the process chain of our clinic facility.

Our highest priority goal is to train our employees to persuade walk-in consumers who arrive at peak times but who do not require immediate care to return at nonpeak times. If we succeed at achieving this goal, we can succeed at eliminating our bottlenecks. So I suppose our nonfinancial indicators should include employee training hours and patient satisfaction scores.

Now let me think about the volume, cost, revenue, and cash flow considerations that appear elsewhere in our business plan. To address those issues, I suppose we should track the number of student workers called to duty during peak times, the amount of time that patients must stand in receptionist lines, and information from our nurses in the treatment areas about the extent to which visits have been shortened (and revenues have been lost) to accommodate high patient volume.

Wow, there isn't a single financial statistic in my entire collection of indicators! But all of these factors drive our financial results in one manner or another, so it's important that we measure them on a daily basis to help us manage our business.

Hugh jots down the following:

- Process chain: Measure training hours, patient satisfaction
- Business plan: Measure student workers, line time, visit length

Looking Forward

In this chapter, we concluded our review of investment value by discussing qualitative and nonfiscal quantitative outcomes measurements that impact the net worth of an organization. This task is important to the development of the business plan because quantitative financial measurements of success (such as those discussed in chapter 15) are not the sole criteria that determine whether organizations are optimizing their value; other criteria must be considered as well.

In the next chapter, we begin our discussion of risk management by discussing scenario event identification activities. In other words, in chapter 17, we move beyond the question, How will we *succeed* at implementing our plan? to address the question, How might we *fail* to implement our plan?

PART VII

Risk Management

CHAPTER 17

Scenario Event Identification

About This Chapter

Chapter 17 begins our review of the risk management section by providing an overview of the discipline and then focusing on its initial activity—in other words, scenario identification. By definition, the risk management section must appear at the end of a business plan because it is designed to help organizations anticipate, prevent, and respond to crises that disrupt plan implementation activities.

Thus, in this chapter, we discuss the four fundamental questions of risk management, each one representing an activity to be undertaken at the conclusion of the planning process. We then proceed to review the activity of scenario event identification; it requires entrepreneurs to anticipate and list all crises that might occur in the future.

Scenario Event Identification

Congratulations on having completed an impressive business plan! However, I'm not ready to put it aside yet. That's because nothing in life ever pans out as expected, and thus we must always be prepared to change our plans when things go wrong. Tell me . . . are you?

You thought that our previous chapter described the last element of our business plan, didn't you?

In a sense, it did. If you have reached this chapter, you have already completed all of the sections of a traditional plan. You have described and analyzed your business model; you have constructed a full set of financial statements from a comprehensive array of volume, cost, and revenue estimates; and you have defined a set of performance outcome measurements. What else is left to plan?

There is, in a sense, nothing left to plan. But aren't you still a bit worried that your plan might fail? All plans fail in some small (or large) way, even the most meticulously researched ones. Sometimes the failure is caused by management error, and sometimes it is caused by factors completely outside of management's control. In either scenario, because some level of failure is inevitable, it behooves us to spend a little time after completing our plan to try to anticipate where we might fail. Then we should try our best to assess whether the cost of that failure can be reduced or eliminated by some proactive action on our part.

The field of business planning that encompasses prospective analyses of failure is called enterprise risk management (ERM). Although a risk management plan is technically a separate assessment of a comprehensive business plan, it is often attached in abbreviated format as an addendum to a business plan.

The Four Questions

How do risk managers practice their craft? To put it simply, they arrive at work each day and ask themselves four basic questions. If they can then supply four relevant answers, they are probably fulfilling their professional responsibilities in a responsible manner. But if they are stumped by at least one question . . . watch out! Problems may ensue.

Let's run through these four questions briefly:

1. *What can go wrong?* Risk managers must keep proverbial laundry lists of every potential significant crisis that might occur in the foreseeable future.
2. *How bad will things get?* Risk managers classify crises as high priority if they are relatively likely to occur and relatively costly if not prevented. They then focus on the highest priority crises.
3. *What will we do if things go wrong?* Risk managers work with operations managers to ensure that the firm's responses in times of crises will be effective if crises cannot be prevented from occurring.
4. *What will we do to prevent things from going wrong?* Risk managers work with operations managers to train employees, test systems, inspect products and services, and audit administrative processes to

try to prevent crises from occurring (or, at the very least, to detect them as soon as they occur).

Questions 3 and 4 are usually addressed simultaneously, but questions 1 and 2 are addressed individually. So let's proceed with our discussion of question 1.

Crisis Identification

What can go wrong? It's a simple question, isn't it? But it's obviously an important one; after all, if we are unable to anticipate our future crises, we will be poorly prepared to *manage* them *if* they occur. Furthermore, we will be unable to attempt to *prevent* them *from* occurring.

At its essence, crisis identification embodies the development of a laundry list of everything that can possibly go wrong in the future. Implicitly embedded in this process is a logical assumption; namely, that we must be willing and able to identify our prospective problems if we are to have any chance of preventing them or responding to them.

"Everything that can possibly go wrong" is a very broad target, though; it may thus be helpful to define standards of materiality below which items may be disregarded as insignificant. It may also be helpful to remind ourselves to focus on the underlying causes of potential crises and not just on their superficial effects. And it may be helpful as well to keep in mind that we must address all relevant issues, including any broad political, economic, social, or technological trends that may affect our organization.

In short, when identifying potential crises, risk managers must review their business plans and ask themselves the following questions: What might go wrong with our plan? Why would it happen? And do I thoroughly understand the root causes of the prospective problem?

Applied Illustration

Hugh awakens one morning and slaps his head. He says, *I've been so focused on our operating divisions that I've forgotten to focus on our support divisions!*

Home care, after all, is a human service business, and thus the human resources and public relations divisions have become the most important support divisions of the agency. The two of them interact with all of the constituents that the operating divisions engage with—consumers, government regulators, funding sources, even managers and employees—on a regular basis.

Hugh decides to jot down a few ideas for the crisis identification section of the business plan to ensure that these departments are focused on the right areas of risk management. He decides to use the topics of politics, economics, society, and technology as a format for structuring his analysis.

Hugh says,

Let's begin with politics. I can divide this topic into two perspectives, one external and one internal. From an external perspective, we are relying heavily on the support of officials in our state and national governments to hold our regulatory working capital requirements at a reasonable level. But we've been hearing rumors lately that they might be considering a series of increases in those requirements. We would need to scramble a bit to come up with additional funds if they increase our fiscal burden there.

And internally, well, our bureaucracy is denser than ever. In fact, we lost a pair of fine young managers last year; they confided in me before they departed that they accepted positions at other institutions because they were frustrated by our internal politics. That's a major problem now, and it can get a lot worse in the future.

Hugh jots down the following:

- Politics—external and internal concerns
- Politicians and internal bureaucrats

Economics? That's the very topic that compelled me to jot down these ideas to begin with! What a mess. We're still using our old econometric and demographic models to decide where to place new business development initiatives and how to focus on emerging opportunities, but none of these models are relevant now. They're based on historical data that is terribly obsolete.

But I need to focus on underlying causes and not superficial effects; I believe that our reliance on these models is just a symptom of a deeper problem. Namely, we need to work harder to maintain closer relationships with the members of our own business community. We need to know which neighborhoods are growing economically and which are contracting; in fact, we even need to anticipate which ones will be growing at some point in the future. By the time these neighborhoods begin to grow rapidly, our competitors have already moved in and established a foothold in the community. By that time, it's too late for us to compete there.

Hugh jots down the following:

- Economics—there's an underlying problem
- Limited knowledge of our own community

Social trends, fortunately, don't really apply to us. A few years ago, a national home care provider with a quirky style and a casual reputation opened an experimental community center, attempting to attract seniors. And today a competitor maintains a few tiny community centers in supermarkets and shopping malls in an attempt to find prospective clients there.

We'll keep an eye on these initiatives, but I don't think they'll explode into full-blown crises for us. Much of our referral volume has now gravitated to electronic media; we haven't had any problems maintaining our relationships with our referral sources.

Hugh jots down the following:

- Society—not a significant concern
- Competitors opening community centers

Our online business, though . . . now that is an important technology concern! We just completed a hugely expensive multiyear Web site development project to launch a wide array of online communication systems, and my chief information officer now tells me that our system might be obsolete within 3 to 5 years. Apparently, the next hot thing is expected to be patient data transmission by mobile telephone, and our system isn't designed to accommodate that.

What a potential boondoggle! It's tempting to simply ignore the situation and hope that mobile telephone data transmissions comes and goes like that experimental community center, but it would be irresponsible for us to bury our heads in the sand. I'll need to remind my risk management department to give this issue a significant amount of attention; I should probably mention it to a couple of our board members as well.

Hugh jots down the following:

- Technology—obsolescence a major problem
- Anticipating mobile telephone data transmissions

Okay, I'll now summarize my short list of things that might go wrong. Those politicians might increase our capital requirements. Our internal bureaucracy might frustrate and drive away our best people. We might grow increasingly out of touch with our local communities. And our technology investment might become worthless if a new generation of mobile hardware devices is adopted by our industry.

Wow, this is interesting. I haven't yet thought about how this ties to our financial projections; I'll get to that when I answer the next risk management question. For now, though, I'll pass along this short list to my public relations and human resources staff and ask them to treat these issues as top priorities. Politicians, employees, community groups, and customers . . . those are the very people that they contact on a daily basis.

Looking Forward

In this chapter, we began our review of the risk management section by focusing on scenario risk identification, the first of four central activities. This task is important to the development of the business plan because organizations must be able to identify potential future crises if they hope to have any chance of managing them in a successful manner.

In the next chapter, we continue our discussion of risk management by discussing the risk assessment function, thereby addressing the second of the four central activities. In other words, in chapter 18, we analyze each scenario event that we have identified, and we assess its propensity to severely damage our organization.

CHAPTER 18

Risk Assessment

About This Chapter

Chapter 18 continues our review of the risk management section by focusing on its second activity—in other words, the activity of risk assessment. Because few organizations possess the resources to address all of the scenarios on their event identification lists, it is necessary to assess each one and then to expend appropriate levels of resources on the highest priority potential crises.

Thus, in this chapter, we describe how event probabilities can be utilized to prioritize among scenarios. We also discuss how expected-value calculations can be utilized to achieve this goal, calculations that encompass both (a) the probability that each event might occur and (b) the resulting impact on the performance of the organization if it does in fact occur.

Risk Assessment

Your crisis identification section was quite unnerving! I'm glad that you took the time to identify all of the risks that confront us, but now we need to focus on the potential crises that may wield the most damage to our business plans. Which areas of your plan are most at risk for failure?

Risk assessment professionals spend their time prioritizing the events that were listed in the previous crisis identification section. No organization can focus on each potential problem with an equal level of intensity; thus, we must focus on the events that pose the greatest risks to our firm.

But how can we prioritize among a universe of unique and disparate problems? There are always political, economic, social, and technological challenges in the *external realm* that must be addressed; these may involve financial, legal, and organizational concerns in our *internal environment* as well. In order to establish priorities among these issues, we must select and implement some reasonable assessment methodology.

Fortunately, the financial statements that we prepare for our business plan provide us with several such methodologies. Publicly traded companies generally use net income as the benchmark for prioritizing various problems; private organizations sometimes opt for operating cash flow instead. And nonprofit organizations use similar statistics such as fund flows and net surpluses.

By using the statistic that we have chosen for assessment purposes, we can apply a decision rule to prioritize among various events. What is our basic rule? To put it simply, the crises that pose the greatest threats to our assessment statistic are given highest priority. And the crises that pose the lesser threats are given lower priority.

Expected Value (EV)

Can it really be that simple? Well, not exactly. There is a significant complication that must be addressed by risk assessment professionals.

The complication, namely, is that *event probabilities* are important. Even though a potential crisis might inflict significant damage, it may not actually occur. And if two different crises are each expected to inflict a similar degree of harm, but if one crisis is twice as likely to occur, then the likelier crisis should be considered the higher priority concern.

In other words, each potential crisis must be assessed in terms of *both* (a) its *probability* of occurrence and (b) its *impact* if it actually occurs. But what if one crisis is highly likely to occur and inflict a moderate amount of damage, and another is moderately likely to occur and inflict a high amount of damage? Which one should be given higher priority?

Our common sense answer is that they may be given equally high priorities; however, some business planners prefer to utilize EVs to prioritize between such events. For instance, if one event is 90% likely to reduce earnings by $10 million, and if another event is 50% likely to reduce earnings by $20 million, then a planner might say that the EV of the first event is $9 million (i.e., 90% of $10 million), and the EV of the second event is $10 million (i.e., 50% of $20 million). The second event would therefore be given slightly higher priority.

In short, when assessing potential crises, risk managers must review their business plans and ask themselves the following questions: Which crises are most likely to occur? Which will cause the most damage if we are unable to prevent them? And based on these assumptions, which events should be given our highest priority?

Applied Illustration

Hugh has received an e-mail message from his corporate controller, an accountant who manages his fiscal services department. The agency's medical malpractice insurance policy is entering its annual renewal period. Hugh prefers to take a lead role in negotiating coverage terms with the insurer that underwrites his contract.

Most of the terms simply carry forward from year to year; there is little or no need to negotiate them with the insurer. But negotiations can become contentious when they address new programs that are still under development and thus have produced limited claims histories.

So Hugh decides to prepare for these negotiations by developing a risk assessment analysis for a program that was initiated less than a year ago. He says,

> *We recently signed a health services contract with a health plan that requires us to provide home-based preventive care visits to patients who have recently been discharged from the cardiology department of a local hospital. Our actuarial advisors informed us that there is a 50% probability of being sued each year under our state's preventive care statutes; if this occurs, we can expect to pay an average of $500,000 per claim in legal costs, settlement fees, or court judgments.*
>
> *Our insurance company is willing to sell us an insurance rider that will cover all of these costs for a premium of $286,000 per year. That seems pretty steep, but it might be worthwhile because our actuaries tell us that there is an additional 0.1% probability each year of having to pay a catastrophic $10 million court judgment if a jury finds us guilty of criminal negligence.*
>
> *So the expected value of this risk, if left uninsured on an annual basis, is $260,000 (i.e., 50% times $500,000, plus 0.1% times $10 million).*

Apparently, we can reduce this value to zero if we spend $286,000 per year to insure it.

Hugh jots down the following:

- EV of risk is $260,000
- Can insure it for $286,000

Then Hugh proceeds to the second risk. He exclaims,

Foreign competition! This once struck us as a relatively unimportant "oddball" issue, but it has recently grabbed our attention. In this program, our referral source of cardiac patients is a major research hospital; we integrate our home-based services with the cardiologists in that institution.

We have recently learned that our health plan has contracted with a cardiology practice in Mexico City to do the same work as our research hospital at a fraction of the cost. Medical costs in the United States are so high that the insurer can pay each patient and a family member to fly to Mexico City, stay in a five-star hotel, and obtain surgical services for far less than what any American provider could possibly charge. And because we don't have a presence in Mexico City, some Mexican home care agency is undoubtedly providing some level of postsurgical care.

At the moment, only a tiny fraction of the insurer's cardiology surgeries are being outsourced to Mexico. But the American research hospital, and a committee of physicians affiliated with the hospital, are working with the health plan to develop a competitive program.

Unfortunately, we haven't been invited to join that working group. So what can we do to address the risk that all of this business might move to Mexico? We have something in mind, but it's an extremely complicated plan. Namely, we can hire Mexican-based nurses and offer the same service. In other words, we can open a foreign branch of our home care agency in Mexico City.

We believe that there is only a 1% chance that we will lose any referral volume this year because of this risk. But if it happens, we may lose the entire program, all $10 million in annual profits. The EV of *this risk may only be $100,000 (i.e., 1% times $10 million), but I'm not even certain that this statistic is comparable to the one addressing our preventive care lawsuit assessment.*

Hugh jots down the following:

- EV of risk is $100,000
- Not insurable and perhaps not comparable on EV terms

Hugh sighs.

Well, which potential crisis is our priority? Based on EV alone, the malpractice issue is worth $260,000 and the foreign issue is worth $100,000, so the malpractice issue would be considered more important. But we can immediately reduce the $260,000 to $0 by signing an insurance policy against loss, whereas the only way to address the $100,000—which might turn out to be a far more catastrophic number—is to spend a significant amount of management time recruiting for nurses in Mexico.

Hmm. I think I might need to throw away these numbers and go with my gut intuition. I'm going to assess each of these issues at an equal level of priority, and I'm going to ask my senior executives to treat them accordingly. Although it's tempting to give the malpractice issue a higher priority because (a) it has a higher EV, and (b) it lends itself to an easy solution, I believe that would be a mistake.

Hugh jots down the following:

- Malpractice issue a higher priority based on EV alone
- Nevertheless, both crises assessed as equal priorities

Looking Forward

In this chapter, we continued our review of the risk management section by focusing on risk assessment, the second of four central activities. This task is important to the development of the business plan because organizations must use a rational methodology (i.e., EV) to prioritize the most risky prospective crises in order to focus appropriate amounts of resources on addressing them.

In the next chapter, we conclude our discussion of risk management by discussing the internal control function, thereby addressing the third and fourth of the four central activities. In other words, in chapter 19, we analyze the scenario events that have been assessed as "highest priorities," and we describe how we must plan to (a) prevent them from occurring and to (b) respond effectively if they do occur.

CHAPTER 19

Internal Control Activities

About This Chapter

Chapter 19 completes our review of the risk management section by focusing on its third and fourth activities—in other words, the activities of crisis prevention and response. Organizations need to focus their risk management activities on preventing crises from occurring and, if they fail to do so, on responding in a timely and effective manner in order to minimize damage.

Thus, in this chapter, we describe how prevention controls, detection controls, and response capabilities can be implemented to address these issues. Such activities are required in order to maximize the probability that entrepreneurs will be able to achieve the goals that are described in the business model, volume estimation, cost estimation, revenue estimation, and investment value sections of the business plan.

Internal Control Activities

I see that you've identified a small number of high priority problems, and now I want to understand how you plan to address them. Can you convince me that you'll be able to prevent these crises, or if that's not possible, that you're well prepared to minimize their effects?

Congratulations! You have now reached the end of the risk management addendum to your business plan. Thus, you have now answered every possible planning question that may be asked by an investor, a banker, a board member, or a regulator.

Nevertheless, you do need to complete one final task; namely, you must describe how you plan to prevent the occurrence of your high priority crises. And if any crises prove to be unavoidable, you must describe how you plan to mitigate the impact on your daily operations.

Even at this late stage of the planning process, it is still possible to conclude that a business concept is not feasible and thus should be rejected. Such an action, although seemingly extreme in nature, is nevertheless appropriate if the activities that you describe in this section are unable to reduce the expected value (EV) of the assessed risks to acceptable and affordable levels.

Three Control Activities

There are three categories of control activities that can be utilized to prevent crises and to minimize their effects. The first two categories are called our internal control activities, while the third is called our crisis response activities.

- *Prevention controls.* These activities are designed to reduce the probabilities that crises will occur at all. Employee training, materials inspection, and production design activities can all be classified as preventive internal controls.
- *Detection controls.* These activities are designed to identify budding crises as soon as they occur and raise red flags so that response capabilities can be implemented. Although they cannot reduce the probabilities that crises will occur in the first place, they can indeed reduce the probabilities that more significant crises may emerge over time. Thus, they may be effective in reducing the impact of any emerging crises on our business plans.
- *Response capabilities.* These activities are designed to contain any damage and minimize the effects of the crises. As with detection controls, however, they too cannot reduce the probabilities that crises will occur in the first place. Likewise, they too may be effective in reducing the impact of emerging crises.

The optimal mix of activities will inevitably vary from organization to organization, from product to product, and from customer segment to customer segment. For instance, how will a manufacturer of children's crayons choose from among these control options? If their customers are unlikely to complain about slight smudges or scuff marks on the crayons, then the manufacturer is unlikely to establish any prevention or detection controls to address this risk. Instead, it may simply establish a toll-free complaint phone number as a response capability and may give away coupons to any who use it.

On the other hand, customers of a luxury automobile dealership are far more likely to complain if their products are even slightly scuffed. Thus, the original manufacturer of the automobiles is likely to rely on prevention control activities in order to avoid any ill will among the dealer's base of customers. And the dealership itself is likely to rely on detection control activities by inspecting the automobiles carefully before selling them to their customers.

Impact on Expected Value (EV)

On a conceptual level, these choices of control activities at children's crayon manufacturers and luxury automobile dealerships make intuitive sense because the expectations of their customer segments are relatively obvious. After all, purchasers of boxes of crayons spend very little money and have no expectations of perfection, whereas purchasers of luxury vehicles spend large sums of money and expect flawless products. It is much more difficult to choose between alternative control activities when customer expectations or other relevant concerns are far less clearly definable.

Under such circumstances, we might need to review the expected value (EV) statistics that we computed in our risk assessment section and estimate the impact of each proposed control activity on the EV of the potential crisis. If we perform this step, we would then select the mix of activities that result in the greatest decline of EVs for the highest priority crises. Of course, we would also need to consider the cost of implementing these activities as well.

When we demonstrate that we are prepared to implement a mix of prevention controls, detection controls, and response capabilities, one that successfully reduces the EVs of high priority crises to acceptable and affordable levels, we create a sense of confidence in our ability to achieve our business goals. Upon the completion of this step, we can finally draw our business planning process to a close.

Applied Illustration

Hugh is the chair of a consortium of local health care providers who are working on behalf of the state government to reduce obesity rates in the region. He is responsible for coordinating the activities of numerous social, educational, cultural, and health care organizations (including his own agency, of course) in order to achieve this goal.

Hugh's state has chosen to reimburse the consortium on a results-driven basis, paying large sums of money to its providers when obesity rates decline to predetermined target levels. The state relies on consumer surveys of weight gains and losses in order to compute obesity rates.

Consortium members feel frustrated because many factors that impact obesity rates fall far outside their control or influence. For instance, when the economy falls into recession, consumers who lose full-time employment often try working two or more part-time, low-paying jobs instead of one in order to maintain their income levels; such consumers often have no time to maintain exercise regimens. In fact, recent increases in obesity rates have been attributed to recessionary conditions that have impacted the local economy.

The consortium has asked Hugh to devise a set of internal controls and response capabilities to address a potential 20% decline in results-driven funding due to a continued decline in local economic conditions. Although the probability of an occurrence of such a decline is only assessed at 10% this year, Hugh estimates that such a decline would blow open a $250,000 hole in the consortium's $1.25 million budget.

Hugh decides to consider each of the three available types of control activities and to select the mix of activities that is most effective in reducing the EV of such a crisis. He begins by estimating this EV at $25,000 (i.e., 10% times $250,000).

Hugh then asks himself,

Is there any way to prevent such a decline in economic conditions and thus exercise regimens? I don't think so, but it may be possible to pass local legislation that installs government-owned exercise equipment in senior centers, community centers, and other public venues. I doubt that my legislators will consider such a proposal seriously, and I can't imagine that it will ever pass into law, but it can't hurt to mention this option in my report to the consortium and assess its probability of success at 0.1%.

It's a lot easier to brainstorm about pragmatic approaches to detect such declines. For instance, instead of waiting until the end of each quarter for the government's health survey results, we could survey a sample of our own consumers on a weekly or monthly basis and ask for their weight figures. Such an approach can hasten our response to increases in obesity rates by a couple of months, thereby reducing the impact of increases in obesity rates by an average of 20%.

But that assumes that we would implement an effective response to an increase in obesity rates; under such circumstances, what would we actually do? Well, I'm sure we'd do what we've always done in the past; namely, we'd step up the frequency and intensity of our health education efforts and visit consumers in their workplaces, homes, and communities. Our historical records indicate that such responses have reduced the severity of increases in obesity rates by an average of 40%.

Hugh jots down the following:

- Probability of success of prevention activity is very low
- Success of detection and response activities is far more likely

So where does that leave us? Well, we know that the full EV of a 20% decline in results-driven funding in the event of a continued recession is $25,000. We do have a potential prevention control, but it reduces our EV by only $25 (i.e., 0.1% of $25,000). Our detection control capability reduces our EV by $5,000 (i.e., 20% of $25,000), and if we then implement our response capability, we'd reduce our EV by another $10,000 (i.e., 40% of $25,000).

So I think we should simply forget about that minor prevention control. If we proceed to implement our detection control and response capability, our EV drops from $25,000 to $10,000. In other words, the damage to our budget as a result of increasing obesity rates (which only has a 10% chance of occurring in the upcoming year) drops from $250,000 to $100,000.

$100,000 is still quite large, but during the past few years, we have been depositing a portion of our revenues into a rainy day fund that now contains $88,000 for such needs. With that in mind, I believe that our control activities will be sufficient to assure our consortium members that we will not need to resort to drastic measures in the face of a severe economic slowdown.

But then Hugh stops himself and takes a deep breath. He says, *Wait a minute. What about the costs of implementing these controls? The detection control simply requires us to gather survey data, but the response capability requires us to make significant expenditures.*

Hugh groans and mutters, *If those expenditures are significant, they might completely offset the benefits that are created by them. Well, I had better check with our leading consortium members in the morning before I finalize my report.*

Hugh jots down the following:

- Rainy day fund covers the residual EV of detection and response activities
- But the cost of the response activity may be prohibitive

Looking Forward

In this chapter, we concluded our review of the risk management section by focusing on internal controls, the third and fourth of the four central planning activities. This task is important to the development of the business plan because organizations must prevent crises from occurring or must mitigate their impact on operations if they do occur in order to achieve the goals that are defined in the business plan.

In the next chapter, we conclude our book with a few final thoughts about the value of management accounting techniques during the development and implementation of business plans. In other words, in chapter 20, we return to the overview of the business planning process that we first described in chapter 1; we then summarize the tasks and activities that we have discussed throughout this book.

PART VIII

Conclusion

CHAPTER 20

Final Thoughts

About This Chapter

Chapter 20 completes our book by emphasizing the importance of reviewing our business plans for completeness and relevance. We also stress that, in volatile business environments, any management plan may become obsolete soon after it is issued; it is therefore important to develop a continuing policy for reviewing and updating its contents.

Thus, in this chapter, we return to the construction metaphor that we first introduced in chapter 1; we utilize it to describe appropriate plan review activities. We also highlight the most important management accounting techniques of each section of the business plan to illustrate how, as an integrated set of activities, they can serve to support and strengthen any plan.

Final Thoughts

Well done! I'm finally convinced that you're ready to manage this organization. But the world changes quickly, and thus elements of your plan became obsolete the moment you completed the final document. So when can I expect your first revision?

Congratulations! Your business plan is now complete, and thus you might wish to stand back for a moment and admire your work. But please don't become complacent; after all, it is now time to begin planning the revisions that you must make to the plan to ensure that it remains relevant under changing circumstances.

As you review your document, please keep in mind that it is more of a work of *science* than a work of *art*. We first mentioned in chapter 1 that we are creating a management accountant's version of a business plan, one that is designed in the style of a sturdy building and not an ethereal sculpture or painting. Although you may have included an occasional flash of brilliant insight in certain sections, most of the details in your plan should strike you as providing relatively mundane—but thoroughly stable and reliable—descriptions of day-to-day business practices.

Let's review, for a moment, the most noteworthy features of your plan. Then we'll proceed to discuss how often, and in what manner, you will need to revise it.

A Building Inspection

Section I, the *business model*, is the foundation upon which the remainder of the plan is constructed. As we review this section, we should ask, is it sufficiently sturdy to withstand the stresses of changing business conditions, or will it fracture under duress? We can be satisfied with your work (a) if the process chain effectively communicates the business strategy, (b) if statistical evidence is presented that clearly supports the key elements of the chain, and (c) if the flexible budget indicates that losses (if any) are affordable even in the worst of times.

Section II, the *volume estimates*, are the frameworks of the walls that are supported by the foundation. *Does each wall fit snugly within its flooring and meet squarely with the adjoining walls?* We can be satisfied with the strength of our volume estimates if we can understand (a) how the production capacity projection is derived from the process flow analysis, (b) how the customer demand projection is established from the demand analysis, and (c) how supply can be reconciled with demand while maintaining reasonable standards of quality.

Section III, the *cost estimates*, are the utility systems that lie within the walls and support the active use of the building. *Does the infrastructure support the operational activities that are required to produce and distribute the product or service?* We can be satisfied with the adequacy of our cost estimates (a) if the direct and indirect costing analysis indicates that expense levels are reasonable in total, (b) if the activity-based costing analysis indicates that expenditure levels are appropriate for each major customer segment, and (c) if the variance analysis indicates that unexpected cost fluctuations can be managed in an effective fashion.

Section IV, the *revenue estimates*, are the finishing details on the walls. *Are the prices that are affixed to products and services attractive to customers? Can they produce sufficient revenues to pay all costs and produce reasonable profits?* We can be satisfied with the sufficiency of our pricing strategy if (a) the cost behavior analysis affirms the reasonableness of the price targets, (b) plans are in place to respond to the pricing decisions of competitors, and (c) contingent discounting strategies can be implemented if price wars become necessary.

Section V, the *investment valuation data*, is the roof that provides shelter for the entire entity. *Is the organization prepared to achieve all of its financial and nonfinancial goals to reward its investors or other sources of capital?* We can be satisfied that investors can support the plan if (a) the cash flow analysis confirms the solvency of the entity, (b) the financial ratio analysis provides indicators of fiscal health, and (c) the dashboard reporting system provides signals of qualitative strength as well.

Section VI, the *risk management analysis*, is actually an addendum to the plan and not a core component of it. *Is the organization prepared to manage emerging crises when they require the abandonment of normal operating procedures?* We can be satisfied that the firm is able to weather such storms if (a) all potential crises are clearly identified, (b) the highest priority problems are appropriately emphasized, and (c) a comprehensive array of internal controls and response activities can effectively reduce the risks of losses to affordable levels.

Revising the Plan

Now that we have completed our review of our plan, how often should we consider revising it? The frequency of our review activities depend on the level of stability within our organization, as well as within our general industry. For firms and industries that rarely experience significant changes, it may be sufficient to revise their business plans every 1 to 3 years. But for firms and industries that are experiencing significant political, economic, social, and technological changes, revisions may be required every quarter or even every month.

With the establishment of this time frame, who should be required to conduct review activities? Unless our organization maintains a full-time strategic planning department, it may be appropriate to ask managers from different divisions to collaborate on these tasks. After all, the operations function continually works with concepts related to the business model, as does the production function regarding volume estimates, the accounting function regarding cost estimates, the marketing function regarding revenue estimates, and the finance function regarding investment valuation issues.

In addition, the risk management function may monitor evolving business conditions inside and outside of the organization. Thus, they may also take the lead in suggesting revisions to the business plan.

Applied Illustration

Hugh has just received some exciting news. Last year, on a whim, he responded to a proposal from the Chinese government to operate a network of home health care agencies throughout that nation . . . and now his proposal has been approved for implementation! So Hugh is now in Beijing, preparing to discuss his business plan with the new employees of his fledgling Asian division.

Hugh picks up the latest copy of his agency's Asian business plan. He says,

> *Let's see if I can use this document to define our Asian strategy in simple and common sense terms.*
>
> *Hmm. Our business model focuses on our ability to bring huge numbers of new consumers into our programs. But I'm not sure whether our process chain gives enough emphasis to the challenges that we face in recruiting large numbers of well trained nurses and therapists.*
>
> *After all, these employees need to sit down and explain our policies and practices to our new consumers. We weren't concerned about recruiting these employees when we first wrote our business plan; we were only expecting to open home care service hubs in one Chinese city per quarter, and we believed that we could easily find sufficient numbers of qualified people to work in them. But now the Chinese government is encouraging us to open five service hubs per quarter, and thus we now face this human resources challenge.*

It's interesting how this one significant challenge affects each of the remaining sections of our business plan. Without qualified nurses to attract consumers by appearing in Chinese community centers, our volume estimates would need to be revised to account for the fact that our demand may be lower than expected. And the costs of employing large numbers of nurses may be onerous if we hire them and then realize that demand has not yet materialized. And that, in turn, may require us to engage in across-the-board price discounting activities to try to entice Chinese consumers to utilize our service. And yet, if we don't address the underlying human resources problem, the resulting issues will never be resolved.

Hugh jots down the following:

- Lack of qualified nurses and therapists is our primary risk
- May lead to lower customer demand, higher costs, and price discounting

So what should we do about it? I suppose we'll need to start training our nurses and therapists about consumer outreach, education, and marketing activities soon after hiring them and not simply assume that they're joining us with the knowledge and skills that are required to attract and maintain our consumer base. It might not be a bad idea to find innovative and culturally appropriate ways to educate our consumers as well; many of them may be totally unfamiliar with the practices of Western business organizations in general and of home health care agencies in particular.

So where does that leave us? I suppose I'll need to reach out to my new Chinese colleagues and ask them for their assistance in updating our business plan in each of these areas. And as my own risk manager, I'll need to create a set of internal controls and response capabilities to implement my recommendations.

I'd love to fly each and every one of our new Chinese hires to our American headquarters for a full immersive month of training, but I know that's simply unaffordable. Perhaps, though, we can fly our

*senior Chinese managers to America for "train the trainer" activities
and then ask them to educate our employees throughout China as a
prevention control activity.*

*And if we ever find out that consumer demand is starting to
decline anyway, we could bite the cost bullet at that time. Perhaps
we'd assign a large team of American trainers to fan out across China
and conduct emergency training activities as a risk response capability.*

Hugh jots down the following:

- Train the trainers to prevent a human resources crisis
- Fly American trainers to China if a "plan B" risk response is
  required

Looking Forward

In this chapter, we concluded our book by explaining how entrepreneurs
should construct and review their business plans. It is always important
to review business plans because, in a rapidly changing business environment, fundamental assumptions and business practices that seem reasonable during one period may become functionally obsolete during the next
period.

In the appendix to this book, we present the business planning outline of a small start-up business that has followed our approach. In other
words, whereas the applied illustrations of the 20 book chapters followed
Hugh's planning activities through various operating and support divisions of his agency, the appendix presents an outline of 20 consecutive
applied illustrations for a business with a single small start-up division.

APPENDIX

A Small Business, Single Division Illustration

About This Chapter

This appendix of our book illustrates all 18 chapters of a business plan (described in chapters 2 through 19 of this text) by applying our material to a small, single division start-up business. Some sections are represented by notes and other sections by data; all sections, though, conclude with a "bottom line" comment to represent the primary conclusion(s) that the entrepreneur drew from the analysis.

Thus, in this chapter, we demonstrate that management accounting principles can be employed to create business plans for any product or service, regardless of the size of the organization that produces it. The following plan represents a brief synopsis of one such plan; actual business plans, of course, can extend for hundreds of pages.

Spokesguy Business Plan

Chapter 2: Defining the Process Chain

Our business model of Spokesguy is to collect subscription revenues from corporate advertisers for managing "urban lifestyle" spokespersons on a continuing basis and at special events. Our Spokesguy employees are a culturally and ethnically diverse group who are well trained (by nature of their urban living and working experience) to understand and execute marketing strategies for global firms. We will establish a "command center" in downtown Manhattan, home of our business and of our corporate advertisers, to directly intervene when our employees need our assistance. We will focus on corporations with a large urban presence who are selling products to native New Yorkers.

By maintaining a very low level of indirect and fixed costs, we hope to become profitable within the year.

The bottom line: Young, diverse, and intelligent Spokesguys with a genuine "urban New York" presence.

Chapter 3: Justifying the Process Chain With Statistical Evidence

We described our business model to 10 local business managers in downtown New York and then asked them, on a scale of 1 to 10, (a) Should a spokesperson for a local business actually live in New York? (b) Should a local spokesperson company charge significantly lower rates than an ad agency? (c) Should a young spokesperson be closely supervised? and (d) How attractive would businesses like yours find our service?

We found that our correlation statistic for (b) is highly significant, for (c) is modestly significant, and for (a) is insignificant. Thus, we decided to emphasize cost and control, thereby going "downmarket."

The bottom line: We can maintain low prices by keeping costs down, remaining local, and avoiding competition.

Chapter 4: Assessing Preliminary Profitability With Flexible Budgets

We are charging $1,000 per day for active attendance at special events and $2,000 per month for passive modeling of clothing and merchandise. We are spending $4,000 per month for a small business office, a telephone system, and marketing materials. And we will pay Spokesguys $1,000 per month (see Table 21.1).

Our private investors have authorized us to spend (or lose) up to $10,000, which would provide us with capital to finance several

Table 21.1.

Monthly	1 passive + 1 active	4 passive + 4 active	10 passive + 10 active
Revenue	$3,000	$12,000	$30,000
Expenses	$5,000	$8,000	$14,000
Net profits	−$2,000	$4,000	$16,000

months of losses in the low volume scenario. The moderate volume scenario may be insufficient to justify the effort required to start up the business, but even if the high volume scenario fails to materialize, we can liquidate the entity and recognize a small gain if we can achieve the moderate volume scenario.

The bottom line: We can earn close to $50,000 in our first year by managing four Spokesguys, an easily achievable target.

Chapter 5: Estimating Supply Capacity With Process Flow Analysis

We will sign each Spokesguy to a contract with an advance of half the first month's compensation prior to signing contracts with customers, thus designating the Spokesguy contracts as direct materials. The employees themselves are the direct laborers, with work-in-process beginning on the first day of the month and ending on the final day of the month. Finished goods are contracts that are completed at the end of the final day of the month and that are considered "final sales" shortly thereafter when the advertiser acknowledges that services have been adequate.

In a typical month, we will begin with four direct material contracts and end with four finished goods and four goods sold. We will need four cell phones (i.e., overhead) to give to the Spokesguys and 4 half days of supervisory time each week (i.e., indirect labor) to oversee employees. These costs can all be easily financed out of the monthly fixed cost budget.

The bottom line: We must maintain a set of Spokesguy contracts at the front end and convert monthly contracts to fast cash at the back end.

Chapter 6: Estimating Customer Demand

We plan to raise brand awareness for our product by asking Spokesguys to walk around the business districts of New York with inexpensive T-shirts that read, "Your ad here!" After saturating our local market with this inexpensive marketing technique, we plan to reinforce our brand message by staging "guerrilla marketing" performances on city streets with local actors and actresses.

With $200 in donated T-shirts and $400 in performance funding expenditures, we expect to generate four to eight customers from the awareness marketing campaign and another four to eight customers from the reinforcement marketing campaign. We can reduce or eliminate the second campaign if the first campaign falls short of expectations, though we may "pull the plug" on the entire initiative if the first campaign generates no leads.

The bottom line: Local, inexpensive viral marketing activities may generate up to four times the volume we need to earn $50,000 in our first year.

Chapter 7: Reconciling Supply and Demand via Quality Management

We can theoretically generate as many as 16 customers from our marketing activities; however, we have only planned to serve as many as 10 customers at a time. We believe that we will be able to extend our production capacity toward 16 by investing in prevention activities (i.e., an employee trainer at $1,000 per month), appraisal activities (i.e., a management assistant at $500 per month), and external failure activities (i.e., a "guaranteed satisfaction or your money back" policy). Although the cost of such activities would reduce our profits, it would not eliminate profits at volumes between 10 and 16.

The bottom line: If we must strain to serve more customers, we can afford to hire additional staff and offer satisfaction guarantees.

Chapter 8: Estimating Direct and Indirect Costs

Because we plan to earn a profit by the end of our first year of operations, we will create a costing schedule for our entire first year. We will begin with direct material for two presigned employee contracts, but we will not require any beginning work in progress or finished goods. And we will end with direct material for four presigned employee contracts with no ending work in progress. However, we expect to have four contracts in finished goods at year-end.

Based on the state of the market, we might need to presign more employees to ensure that they are available at an earlier time, thereby increasing the size and financial burden of our direct material. On the other hand, we might be able to eliminate our finished goods by reducing or eliminating the possibility that our customers might take advantage of our money back guarantee.

The bottom line: The costs of maintaining Spokesguy contracts at the front end are significant but not onerous.

Chapter 9: Assessing Cost Structures With Activity-Based Costing

We are charging customers differential prices for monthly subscriptions and daily special events, thereby removing much of the pricing risk from our business model. It will probably be necessary, though, to place a "cap" (perhaps two special events per month) on our Spokesguy appearances.

We are planning to staff our own "command center" and will be paying ourselves out of profits, thereby removing much of the cost risk associated with activity-based costing. However, we might wish to calculate the cost of "extremely difficult to manage Spokesguys," and if necessary we might wish to add a line to our cost structure that compensates ourselves for excessive activity.

The bottom line: We are prepared to cap our costly "special event" service and implement premium pricing policies if necessary.

Chapter 10: Risk Management With Cost Variance Analysis

Our standard direct material budget calls for payments to four Spokesguys over the course of the year. However, if the Spokesguys unexpectedly demand higher fees, we might need to increase our average payments while maintaining a total of four employees. Under such circumstances, although the direct material quantity variance would be zero, we would be incurring a direct material rate variance. Nevertheless, we believe that the additional cost would be controllable and affordable.

Furthermore, if two of our four Spokesguys unexpectedly quit and need to be replaced at the last moment by multiple (and far more expensive) employees, we might need to increase our rate while increasing our quantity from four to six. Nevertheless, we again believe that the additional cost would be controllable and affordable.

The bottom line: We understand that labor turnover and compensation is inherently unstable; these risks appear to be manageable.

Chapter 11: Price Targeting on the Basis of Cost Behavior

With a $3,000 unit price, $1,000 unit variable costs, and $4,000 total fixed costs, we break even at a volume of $4,000/$2,000 = 2 units. However, our conservative target (monthly) profit for our first year is $4,000, which can be achieved with a volume of [$4,000 + $4,000]/$2,000 = 4 contracts. We believe that 4 contracts is well within the range of achievability.

The bottom line: *Our break-even target volume of two contracts represents an easily achievable goal, while our $50,000 target profit volume of four contracts represents a moderately achievable goal.*

Chapter 12: Competitive Pricing via Game Theory

We acknowledge that advertising agencies in the New York region could conceivably compete for our business. However, given our "downmarket" emphasis and extremely low fixed-cost structure, we believe that such competition is unlikely.

On the other hand, competitors that are based in other neighborhoods in the New York region could easily compete for our business as well. If these rivals challenge us for our customers, a "hold prices firm while remaining in our home turf" strategy may yield mutually superior outcomes to a "slash prices while invading our rival's home turf" strategy. In other words, we might be better off remaining in Manhattan at our current price levels and ceding the remainder of the city to competitors in the outer boroughs while remaining fully prepared to slash prices and invade other boroughs if challenged to do so, all the while respecting the laws of fair competition, of course.

The bottom line: *Our pricing power is strong if we remain local, and we are prepared to protect our "turf" from competitors.*

Chapter 13: Price-Discounting Strategies

If a single customer demands a discount, we might be willing to charge him or her a price as low as $1,000.01 per month. However, we would only accept such a low price if that customer promised to refer to us (through word of mouth) to two or three other customers who are willing to pay our full standard price.

If a competitor invades our home turf, we might be willing to slash average prices "across the board" to as little as $8,000/4 = $2,000 when four Spokesguys are employed and $14,000/10 = $1,400 when 10 Spokesguys are employed. In fact, we might create discounting strategies that offer free Spokesguy appearances at special events in order to lock in subscription revenue, thereby reducing the average price level accordingly.

The bottom line: We can slash average monthly revenue per customer and still survive; we are prepared to do so if necessary.

Chapter 14: Cash Flow Analysis

With little inventory, no major fixed asset requirements, and no debt financing repayments, we project that operating cash flow and total cash flow will both be positive during our first year of operations. There is a possibility, though, that we may be faced with customers paying late, leading to an increase in accounts receivable that will cause a decline in cash balances.

Therefore, we will adhere to a strict 30-day collection policy that will terminate services after 1 month if outstanding invoices are not paid in full. Although such a policy might limit our ability to sell services to customers who are accustomed to longer terms, we believe that the danger of cash flow insolvency is so great that this restriction on growth is appropriate.

The bottom line: We are willing to "cut off" nonpaying customers very quickly to maintain cash flow solvency.

Chapter 15: Financial Ratio Analysis

Although we do not require start-up capital per se, our private investors have authorized us to spend (or lose) up to $10,000, and thus we consider $10,000 to be our initial investment. They have informed us that the minimal required return on investment for this relatively low risk venture is 15%, and the average expected return is 30%.

If we earn the $4,000 in profits predicted by our flexible budget, the minimum residual income will be +$2,500 and the maximum residual income will be +$1,000. Thus, we believe that our investors will be delighted with the fiscal results that we will produce for them.

A return on equity (ROE) ratio similarly projects very satisfactory returns on equity. We expect to earn relatively large amounts of revenue and net income on relatively small "bases" of total assets, thereby producing an extremely healthy ratio of sales to assets and relatively healthy percentages for the ratio of assets to equity, as well as the ratio of profits to sales.

The bottom line: With few assets and low costs, our ROE will be heavily influenced by the ratio of sales to assets.

Chapter 16: Outcomes Management and Measurement

Although the process chain framework described at the beginning of this document appears to be valid, in retrospect, our high degree of profitability might lead us to conclude that our emphasis on "downmarket" low cost business may eventually prove to be unnecessary. In fact, if we competitively focus on the Manhattan business markets to avoid destructive outer borough competition, we might be able to sell our services to a more upscale clientele.

Nevertheless, we believe that a more upscale approach should only be attempted after we establish our business during our first year and earn a profit that can then be reinvested in expansion activities. In order to establish our business, we intend to track the following key performance indicators: (a) employee performance statistics that are collected through surveys of the individuals who encounter our Spokesguys on the street, (b) command center oversight performance statistics that are collected through a complaint reporting process, (c) customer satisfaction performance statistics that are collected through feedback surveys, and (d) profit outcomes that are tracked through monthly and quarterly financial accounting reports.

The bottom line: We will rely on feedback surveys and focus on the local downscale market but we may go upscale in the future.

Chapter 17: Scenario Event Identification

The preceding chapters of the business plan note several potential problems that may be designated as event scenarios. For instance, chapter 8 refers to the risk that we may not be able to presign a sufficient number of Spokesguys to contracts to meet demand. And chapters 12 and 13 refer to the risk that competitors may attempt to raid our customer base, forcing us to consider slashing prices to retain them.

The bottom line: The first risk event scenario refers to an unstable and unreliable internal employee pool, while the second and third risk event scenarios refer to the possibility of external competition.

Chapter 18: Risk Assessment

The cost of the first risk event scenario is one or more lost customer(s). With a $3,000 unit price and $1,000 unit variable cost, the cost of each lost customer is $2,000. If there is a 10% probability of one lost customer under this risk event scenario, it would possess an EV of $200.

The cost of the second and third risk event scenarios is a complete loss of all profits if a price war erupts and we slash our profits to a break-even level. If we are serving 16 customers when that occurs, and thus (before considering fixed costs) are earning $16,000 in monthly profits, the impact of such a scenario would be a complete loss of $16,000. Even if there is only a 5% probability that such a price war would occur, the expected value (EV) of this risk event scenario would be $800.

The bottom line: The possibility of a price war represents the highest priority risk event scenario.

Chapter 19: Internal Control Activities

The most effective strategy for preventing a price war is to attempt to focus on segments of the market that feature limited competition. For instance, we might join local business associations and industry groups to learn about the target customer markets of our potential competitors; we might then attempt to avoid focusing our expansion plans on those areas.

If a price war cannot be avoided, then we will need to detect aggressive actions by rivals as soon as they occur. We might thus ask our customers to let us know if they receive any aggressive price promotion literature, or other aggressive proposals, from our rivals.

Finally, if we detect such aggressive actions, we will need to respond by deeply discounting our prices as we discussed in chapter 13 of this plan. Although that may result in the complete loss of our profits for a period of time, we believe that it would be wise to implement such a response in order to preserve our customer base.

The bottom line: A mix of prevention, detection, and response activities would best serve our purposes.

Looking Forward

In this chapter, we provided an applied illustration of a business plan outline, one that utilized our management accounting techniques to develop a plan for a small business with a single division.

Now that you have reached the conclusion of our text, we hope that you are looking forward to applying our management accounting techniques to your own organization. We wish you success and great fortune as you endeavor to achieve your goals.

Index